The
HIDDEN PLACES
of
SUFFOLK

Edited by
Peter Long

© Travel Publishing Ltd. 1998

Published by:
Travel Publishing Ltd
7a Apollo House, Calleva Park
Aldermaston, Berks, RG7 8TN

ISBN 1-902-00725-5

© Travel Publishing Ltd 1998

First Published:	*1989*	*Fifth Edition:*	*1998*
Second Edition:	*1992*		
Third Edition:	*1994*		
Fourth Edition:	*1996*		

Regional Titles in the Hidden Places Series:

Cambridgeshire & Lincolnshire	Channel Islands
Cheshire	Cornwall
Devon	Dorset, Hants & Isle of Wight
Essex	Gloucestershire
Heart of England	Highlands & Islands
Kent	Lake District & Cumbria
Lancashire	Norfolk
Northeast Yorkshire	Northumberland & Durham
North Wales	Nottinghamshire
Peak District	Potteries
Somerset	South Wales
Suffolk	Surrey
Sussex	Thames & Chilterns
Warwickshire & W Midlands	Welsh Borders
Wiltshire	Yorkshire Dales

National Titles in the Hidden Places Series:

England	Ireland
Scotland	Wales

Printing by: Nuffield Press, Abingdon

Cartography by: Estates Publications, Tenterden, Kent

Line Drawings: Sarah Bird

Editor: Peter Long

Cover : Clare Hackney

Born in 1961, Clare was educated at West Surrey College of Art and Design as well as studying at Kingston University. She runs her own private water-colour school based in Surrey and has exhibited both in the UK and internationally. The cover is taken from an original water-colour of the green at Cavendish.

Foreword

The Hidden Places series is a collection of easy to use travel guides taking you, in this instance, on a relaxed but informative tour through Suffolk, a county blessed with incomparable rural beauty encompassing wide open spaces broken by gentle hills, and rivers which meander to a coastline teeming with wildlife. Our books contain a wealth of interesting information on the history, the countryside, the towns and villages and the more established places of interest. But they also promote the more secluded and little known visitor attractions and places to stay, eat and drink many of which are easy to miss unless you know exactly where you are going.

We include hotels, inns, restaurants, public houses, teashops, various types of accommodation, historic houses, museums, gardens, garden centres, craft centres and many other attractions throughout Suffolk. Most places have an attractive line drawing and are cross-referenced to coloured maps found at the rear of the book. We do not award merit marks or rankings but concentrate on describing the more interesting, unusual or unique features of each place with the aim of making the reader's stay in the local area an enjoyable and stimulating experience.

Whether you are visiting the area for business or pleasure or in fact are living in the county we do hope that you enjoy reading and using this book. We are always interested in what readers think of places covered (or not covered) in our guides so please do not hesitate to use the reader reaction forms provided to give us your considered comments. We also welcome any general comments which will help us improve the guides themselves. Finally if you are planning to visit any other corner of the British Isles we would like to refer you to the list of other *Hidden Places* titles to be found at the rear of the book.

Suffolk Location Map

Contents

CHAPTER ONE
Northwest Suffolk

Market Cross, Mildenhall

Chapter 1 - Area Covered

For precise location of places please refer to the colour maps found at the rear of the book.

1
Northwest Suffolk

Introduction

Cambridgeshire, Norfolk, the A134 and the A14 frame this northern part of West Suffolk, which includes Bury St Edmunds, a pivotal player in the country's religious history, and Newmarket, one of the major centres of the horseracing world. Between and above them are picturesque villages, bustling market towns, rich farming countryside, the fens, and the expanse of sandy heath and pine forest that is Breckland. Before the forests were developed the area was sometimes known as the Great East Anglian Desert. The forest is the work of the Forestry Commission, who planted the first pines in 1922 and gradually reduced the area of heathland. Rabbits were practically the only inhabitants when the work began, and the Commission had to destroy 83,000 of them before planting their first 6,000 acres. Country parks, nature reserves and heritage centres bring wildlife and history into fascinating focus, and the region is among the most abundant in the land in antiquities and signs of thousands of years of civilisation.

When the Roman Empire collapsed in the 5th century Britain was settled by Angles and Saxons from Germany and Jutes from Denmark. England was divided into several kingdoms and East Anglia, of which Suffolk was part, was ruled by the family of Wuffinga.

The wealth, trade and culture of those times is gradually being unearthed, mainly in Suffolk. The early Anglo-Saxon period ran from the 5th to the 7th century AD and is seen at West Stow and a few other places, mainly in burial grounds. The conversion to Christianity begain in the 7th century when Bishop Felix started to establish monasteries. Most of the early Anglo-Saxon settlements were deserted in the 7th century and little is known of the 8th and 9th centuries. Many of the remains of the Anglo-Saxon period are on display, notably, in this Chapter, at West Stow and in Bury St Edmunds (Abbey ruins and Moyses Hall) and elsewhere in Blythburgh, Sutton Hoo and Snape, and in museums in Ipswich and Woodbridge.

The most recent 'invasion' was of a non-colonising nature, namely the Americans, who arrived in force in the county in 1942. Air bases sprang up all over Suffolk (19 in all) and several of them still display memorials of their visits. John Appleby was the most notable American visitor, falling in love with Suffolk and recording his cycling explorations in his book *Suffolk Summer*. The royalties of that book contribute to the upkeep of the rose garden in Bury St Edmunds, where another transatlantic bond stands in the shape of a seat fashioned from the frame of a Flying Fortress. Two of the Suffolk USAAF bases are still operational, at Mildenhall and Lakenheath, but many other fields are still visible, along with several control towers and memorials in local churches. The most notable collection of memorabilia is in the Aviation Museum at Flixton, near Bungay (see Chapter 4).

Newmarket

On the western edge of Suffolk, Newmarket is home to some 16,000 human and 3,000 equine inhabitants. The historic centre of British racing lives and breathes horses, with 60 training establishments, 50 stud farms, the top annual thoroughbred sales and two racecourses (the only two in Suffolk). Thousands of the population are involved in the trade, and racing art and artefacts fill the shops, galleries and museums; one of the oldest established saddlers even has a preserved horse on display - *'Robert the Devil'*, runner-up in the 1880 Derby.

History records that Queen Boadicea of the Iceni, to whom the six-mile Devil's Dyke stands as a memorial, thundered around these parts in her lethal chariot behind her shaggy-haired horses and she is said to have established the first stud here. In medieval times the chalk heathland was a popular arena for riders to display their skills and in 1605 James I paused on a journey north to enjoy a spot of hare coursing. He enjoyed the place and said he would be back; in

Newmarket Races

moving the royal court to his Newmarket headquarters he began the royal patronage which has remained strong down the years. Charles I maintained the royal connection but it was Charles II who really put the place on the map when he, too, moved the Royal court in the spring and autumn of each year. He initiated the Town Plate, a race which he himself won twice as a rider and which, in a modified form, still exists.

One of the racecourses, the ***Rowley Mile***, takes its name from Old Rowley, a favourite horse of the Merry Monarch. Here the first two classics of the season, the 1,000 and 2,000 Guineas, are run, together with important autumn events including the Cambridgeshire and the Cesarewich. There are some 16 race days at this track, while on the leafy July course, with its delightful garden-party atmosphere, a similar number of race days takes in all the important summer fixtures.

The visitor to Newmarket can learn almost all there is to know about flat racing and racehorses by making the grand tour of the several establishments which are open to the public (sometimes by appointment only). ***The Jockey Club***, which was the first governing body of the sport and until recently the ultimate authority, was formed in the middle of the 18th century and occupies an imposing building which was restored and rebuilt in Georgian style in the 1930s. Originally a social club for rich gentlemen with an interest in the turf, it soon became the all-powerful regulator of British racing, owning all the racing and training land. When holding an enquiry the stewards sit round a horseshoe table and the jockey or trainer under scrutiny faces them on a strip of carpet by the door - hence the expression 'on the mat'.

Next to the Jockey Club in the High Street is the *National Horseracing Museum*. Opened by The Queen in 1983, its five galleries chronicle the history of the Sport of Kings from its royal beginnings through to the top trainers and jockeys of today. Visitors can ride a mechanical horse, try on racing silks, record a race commentary, ask awkward questions and enjoy a snack in the café, whose walls are hung with murals of racing personalities. The chief treasures among the art collection are equine paintings by Alfred Munnings, while the most famous item is probably the skeleton of the mighty Eclipse, whose superiority over his contemporaries gave rise to the saying *'Eclipse first, the rest nowhere'*.

A few steps away is *Palace House*, which contains the remains of Charles II's palace and which, as funds allow, is being restored for use as a visitor centre and museum. In the same street, and still standing, is *Nell Gwynn's house*, which some say was connected beneath the street to the palace. The diarist John Evelyn spent a night in (or on?) the town during a royal visit and declared the occasion to be *"more resembling a luxurious and abandoned rout than a Christian court"*. The palace is the new location for the Newmarket Tourist Information Centre. Other must-sees on the racing enthusiast's tour are *Tattersalls*, where leading thoroughbred sales take place from April to December; the *British Racing School*, where top jockeys are taught the ropes; the *National Stud*, open from March till August plus race days in September and October (booking essential); and the *Animal Health Trust* based at Lanwades Hall, where a Visitor Centre has recently opened. The National Stud at one time housed no fewer than three Derby winners - Blakeney, Mill Reef and Grundy.

Horses aren't all about racing, however. One type of horse you won't see in Newmarket is the wonderful Suffolk Punch, a massive yet elegant working horse which can still be seen at work at Rede Hall Park Farm near Bury St Edmunds and at Kentwell Hall in Long Melford (see under those locations). All Punches descend from Crisp's horse, foaled in 1768. The Punch is part of the Hallowed Trinity of animals at the very centre of Suffolk's agricultural history; the others are the Suffolk Sheep and the Red Poll Cow. And it is entirely appropriate that the last railway station to employ a horse for shunting wagons should have been at Newmarket. That hardworking one-horse-power shunter retired in 1967, the same year that his patrician cousin and fellow Newmarket resident Royal Palace was steaming home in the 2,000 Guineas and the Derby.

Newmarket has things to offer the tourist outside the equine world, including the churches of *St Mary and All Saints*, and *St Agnes*, and a landmark at each end of the High Street - a Memorial Fountain in honour of Sir Daniel Cooper and the Jubilee Clock Tower commemorating Queen Victoria's Golden Jubilee.

A horseracing atmosphere fills *The Yard* (formerly called The Grosvenor), whose position in an alley just off the main street ensures peace plus accessibility. Sheila and Jeff Watt are the tenants, and it's Sheila who cooks all the food - curries, chili, pies and an excellent Sunday lunch when you can really taste the gravy. Barbecues take place in the beer garden, and the good food is accompanied by well-kept beers and a selection of wines. Racing folk are naturally in their element, with both a big TV screen to see where their money went and rooms that are literally crammed with turf memo-

The Yard

rabilia: paintings of racing scenes by local artists, silks and caps and saddles, feed trays and brasses and bridles, signs and trophies, rollcalls of major race winners, a vets corner with authentic accessories displayed behind glass, even a cart hanging above the bar. Apart from the geegees, there's always something to entertain here, with spontaneous fun evenings throughout the year (everyone dresses up for the Abba nights!) and a variety of pub games to play. *The Yard, Grosvenor Yard, Newmarket, Suffolk, CB8 9AW. Tel: 01638 662220*

Warren Hill Cottage was originally two cottages, part of the railway complex where horses would arrive from the north for Newmarket races. The two cottages are now joined into one, making the

Warren Hill Cottages

most delightful spot for an overnight stay. The friendly owner, Vicky Ward, is herself involved in the bloodstock business and many of her guests are here for the races, the sales and her expertise. Two single and one double bedroom are in the main building, while another double, completely self-contained, is in the garden, which runs down to a large grassy area and a horse exercise pen. The atmosphere is wonderfully relaxed, with guests having the run of the house. The cottage lies between the training establishments of John Gosden and Sir Michael Stoute. *Warren Hill Cottage, 27 Bury Road, Newmarket, Suffolk, CB8 7BY. Tel: 01638 661103*

Around Newmarket

Westley Waterless   *Map 1 ref A6*
5 miles S of Newmarket off the B1061

Vivien Galpin's **Westley House** is a family home with dogs in the house and horses in the paddock. Dating from the 17th century and rebuilt around 1783, it was formerly the rectory for the little village of Westley Waterless, which lies in peaceful countryside (actually

Westley House

in Cambridgeshire) five miles south of Newmarket. Visitors are welcomed as paying guests, and overnight accommodation comprises two twin bedrooms and two singles, all spacious, traditional in style, carpeted throughout and offering delightful views. They share two bathrooms. A large, well-furnished drawing room, opening on to the garden, is reserved for guests. Breakfast is served in the dining room, and an evening meal can be arranged with prior notice. Check directions when booking. *Westley House, Westley Waterless, Near Newmarket, Suffolk, CB8 0RQ. Tel: 01638 508112*

Exning   *Map 1 ref A5*
2 miles NW of Newmarket on the A14

A pause is certainly in order at this ancient village, whether on a trip out of Newmarket or arriving from Cambridgeshire on the A14. Anglo-Saxons, Romans, the Iceni and the Normans were all here, and the Domesday Book records the village under the name of Esselinga. The village was stricken by a plague during the Iceni occupation, so its market was moved to the next village. Thus Newmarket acquired its name. Exning's written history begins when Henry II granted the manor to the Count of Boulogne, who divided it between four of his knights. References to them and to subsequent Lords of the Manor are to be found in the little **Church of St Martin**, which might well have been founded by the Burgundian Christian missionary monk St Felix in the 7th century. Water from the well used by that saint to baptise members of the Saxon royal family is still used for similar ceremonies by the current vicar.

The A14 is a busy main road, but pulling away from the traffic and spending time around this village will be rewarded by some quiet, pleasant walks.

Kentford   *Map 1 ref B5*
5 miles E of Newmarket by the A14

At the old junction of the Newmarket-Bury road stands the grave of a young boy who hanged himself after being accused of sheep-stealing. It was a well-established superstition that suicides should be buried at a crossroads to prevent their spirits from wandering. Flowers are still sometimes laid at the **Boys Grave**, sometimes by punters hoping for good luck at Newmarket races.

Sally Aldous runs **The Cock**, a country pub with a long and interesting history. The oldest parts date from the 13th century and

The Cock

some of the original beams are still to be seen. A priest hole was discovered behind a fireplace in the 1960s, and low beams display more unusual and intricate carvings. These grand old inns often have an interesting collection, and in the case of the Cock it's banknotes on show behind the bar. In the restaurant area, which was once the stable block and coachhouse, a long menu of hot and cold dishes is served lunchtime and evening; the speciality cuisine is Mexican, with enchiladas, fajitas and chimichangas finding favour with the punters. This is racing country and many of the regulars are avid followers of the turf. *The Cock, Bury Road, Kentford, Near Newmarket, Suffolk, CB8 7PR. Tel: 01638 750360*

Moulton
Map 1 ref B5
4 miles E of Newmarket on the B1085

This most delightful village lies in wonderful countryside on chalky downland in farming land and its proximity to Newmarket is apparent from the racehorses which are often to be seen on the large green. The River Kennett flows through the green, before running north to the Lark, a tributary of the Ouse. Flint walls are a feature of many of the buildings, but the main point of interest is the 15th century 4-arch packhorse bridge on the way to the church. A gentle walk east of Moulton brings the visitor to *Gazeley*, which boasts a stud farm, a smithy and, most notably, a 14th century church. Its bells, which still exist but are no longer hung, were once rung to celebrate the failure of the Gunpowder Plot, and also pealed the start of harvesting and any deaths in the village.

Dalham
Map 1 ref B5
5 miles E of Newmarket on the B1063

Eighty per cent of the buildings are thatched (the highest proportion in Suffolk) and there are many other attractions in this pretty village. Above the village on one of the county's highest spots stands *St Mary's Church*, which dates from the 14th century. Its spire toppled over during the gales which swept the land on the night that Cromwell died, and was replaced by a tower in 1627. Sir Martin Stutteville was the leading light behind this reconstruction and an inscription at the back of the church notes that the cost was £400. That worthy's grandfather was Thomas Stutteville, whose memorial near the altar declares that "*he saw the New World with Francis Drake*". (Drake did not survive that journey - his third to South America.) Thomas's grandson died in the fullness of his years (62 wasn't bad for those times!) while hosting a jolly at The Angel Hotel, Bury St Edmunds.

Dalham Hall was constructed in the first years of the 18th century at the order of the Bishop of Ely, who decreed that it should be built up until Ely Cathedral could be seen across the fens on a clear day. That view was sadly cut off in 1957 when a fire shortened the hall to two storeys. Wellington lived here for some years, and much later it was bought by Cecil Rhodes, who unfortunately died before taking up residence. His brother Francis erected the village hall in the adventurer's memory, and he himself is buried in the churchyard.

Another link with the past survives in a **windmill** (sadly minus its sails) that stands behind the pub. The ruins of a second mill (whose sails turned, unusually, to the left) and the original church can be seen on the way from Dalham to Ashley. The final point of interest is the **old maltings**, a conical brick building opposite the turning to the church. More information on windmills is contained in the introduction to Chapter 3.

All in all, Dalham is a place of charm and interest, clearly unlike the one described in *The Times* in the 1880s as full of ruffians and drunks, where the vicar felt obliged to give all the village children boxing lessons to increase their chances of survival.

Owner Dominic Jacombs, an impressive figure standing not far short of 7 feet tall, heads the team at **The Affleck Arms**, a pretty Elizabethan inn at the heart of a quintessential Suffolk village by

The Affleck Arms

the River Kennett. Most of the buildings (and the pub itself) are thatched, and several little footbridges straddle the river. The Affleck family were among the most distinguished residents (a number of generations owned the manor) and the outside walls of the church display monuments to some of their faithful servants, including one to "*a punctual poultry-woman*". Dominic is not only the owner but also the chef, and his bar meals, served lunchtime and evening seven days a week, span a wide range and include a children's menu and a weekday pensioner's lunch. The three eating areas offer one for non-smokers, and fresh flowers or candles on each table reinforce the friendly, welcoming atmosphere. The pub has ample parking, a games room (bar billiards and others), a beer garden and a pets corner to keep the children happy. *The Affleck Arms, 1 Brookside, Dalham, Near Newmarket, Suffolk, CB8 8TG. Tel: 01638 500306*

Mildenhall
Map 1 ref B4

8 miles NE of Newmarket off the A11

On the edge of the Fens and Breckland, Mildenhall is a town which has many links with the past. It was once a port for the hinterland of West Suffolk, though the River Lark has long ceased to be a trade route. Most of the town's heritage is recorded in the excellent

Market Cross, Mildenhall

Mildenhall & District Museum in King Street. Here will be found exhibits of local history (including the distinguished RAF and USAAF base), crafts and domestic skills, the natural history of the Fens and Breckland and, perhaps most famously, the *'Mildenhall Treasure'*. This was a cache of 34 pieces of 4th century Roman silverware - dishes, goblets and spoons - found by a ploughman in 1946 at Thistley Green and now on display in the British Museum. There is evidence of much earlier occupation than the Roman era, with flint tools and other artefacts being unearthed in 1988 on the site of an ancient lake.

The parish of Mildenhall is the largest in Suffolk so it is perhaps fitting that it should boast so magnificent a parish church as **St Mary's**, built of Barnack stone; it dominates the heart of the town and indeed its west tower commands the flat surrounding countryside. Above the splendid north porch (the largest in Suffolk) are the arms of Edward the Confessor and of St Edmund. The chancel, dating back to the 13th century, is a marvellous work of architecture, but pride of place goes to the east window, divided into seven vertical lights. Off the south aisle is the Chapel of St Margaret, whose altar, itself modern, contains a medieval altar stone. At the west end, the font, dating from the 15th century, bears the arms of Sir Henry Barton, who was twice Lord Mayor of London and whose tomb is located on the south side of the tower. Above the nave and aisles is a particularly fine hammerbeam roof whose outstanding feature is the carved angels. Efforts of the Puritans to destroy the angels failed, but traces of buckshot and arrowheads have been found embedded in the woodwork.

Sir Henry North built a manor house on the north side of the church in the 17th century and his successors included a dynasty of the Bunbury family who were Lords of the Manor from 1747 to 1933. Sir Henry Edward Bunbury was the man chosen to let Napoleon Bonaparte know of his exile to St Helena, but the best known member of the family is Sir Thomas, who in 1780 tossed a coin with Lord Derby to see whose name should be borne by a race to be inaugurated at Epsom. Lord Derby won, but Sir Thomas had the satisfaction of winning the first running of the race with his colt Diomed.

The other focal point in Mildenhall is the Market Place, with its 16th century timbered cross.

West Row is a couple of miles west of Mildenhall, from where **The White Horse** attracts many of its customers, including servicemen from the huge air base. The pub is owned and run by Queenie Howard and Lionel Deadman, who was a stockman before adopting

The White Horse

the life of a publican. There are two bars with mock beams on low ceilings, while outside an adventure area in a fenced garden makes it an ideal spot for families. Sports, both indoor and out, are a major feature: a fishing contest on the River Lark is organised here, while cribbage, darts and karaoke all have their weekly slots. *The White Horse, Beechers Road, West Row, Mildenhall, Suffolk, IP28 8NP. Tel: 01638 715828*

Around Mildenhall

Barton Mills
Map 1 ref B4

1 mile S of Mildenhall off the A11

Known as Barton Parva (Little Barton) in Saxon times, the village changed its name during the 18th century. St Mary's Church can trace its origins back to at least 1150, and one of its early rectors had the Pope as his patron. Sir Alexander Fleming had a country house in the village and it is possible that he worked on the invention of penicillin in a shed in the garden.

Worlington
Map 1 ref A4

2 miles W of Mildenhall on the B1102

A small village near the River Lark, known chiefly as the location of **Wamil Hall**, an Elizabethan mansion which stands on the riverbank. Popular lore has it that a person called Lady Rainbow haunts the place, though the spot she favoured for appearances, a flight of stairs, was destroyed in one of the many fires the mansion has suffered. Cricket is very much part of the village scene (there's a splendid village green) and has been since the early days of the last century.

Lakenheath   *Map 1 ref B3*
5 miles N of Mildenhall on the B1112

A sizeable village which is mentioned in the Domesday Book and was once an important place for trade. The main point of interest for the visitor is **St Mary's Church**, notable for an elaborately carved 13th century font, a cambered tie-beam and a set of 15th century benches, carved with eccentric designs of acrobats, fishes and tigers. Lakenheath was the setting for Charles Wesley's first Methodist sermon in the area (1754), and many relatives of Lord Kitchener are buried in the churchyard. RAF Lakenheath, an important air base, stands to the south east of the village. Many significant archaeological finds have come to light in this area, the last as recently as 1997.

Brandon   *Map 1 ref C2*
9 miles NE of Mildenhall on the A1065

On the edge of **Thetford Forest** by the Little Ouse, Brandon was long ago a thriving port, but flint is what really put it on the map. The town itself is built mainly of flint, and flint was mined from early Neolithic times to make arrowheads and other implements and weapons of war. The gun flint industry brought substantial wealth, and a good flint-knapper could produce up to 300 gun flints in an hour. The invention of the percussion cap killed off much of their work so they turned to shaping flints for church building and ornamental purposes. *The Heritage Centre*, in a former fire station in George Street, provides visitors with a splendid insight into this industry, while for an even more tangible feel a visit to **Grimes Graves**, just over the Norfolk border, reveals an amazing site covering 35 acres and 300 pits (one of the shafts is open for visits). With the close proximity of numerous warrens and their rabbit population, the fur trade also flourished here, and that, too, along with forestry, is brought to life in the Heritage Centre.

The whole of this north west corner of Suffolk, know as **Breckland**, offers almost unlimited opportunities for touring by car, cycling or walking. A mile south of town on the B1106 is ***Brandon Country Park***, a 30-acre landscaped site with a tree trail, forest walks, a walled garden and a visitor centre. There's also an orienteering route leading on into Thetford Forest, Britain's largest lowland pine forest. *The High Lodge Forest Centre*, by Santon

Downham (off the B1107), also attracts with walks, cycle trails and adventure facilities.

Elveden   *Map 1 ref C3*
5 miles S of Brandon on the A11

The road from Brandon leads south through the forest to a historic estate village with some unusual architectural features. Where the three parishes of Elveden, Eriswell and Icklingham meet a tall war memorial in the form of a Corinthian column is a landmark.

Elveden Hall became more remarkable than its builders intended when Prince Duleep Singh, heir to the throne of the Punjab, a noted sportsman and shot, and the man who handed over the Koh-I-Noor diamond to Queen Victoria, arrived on the scene. Exiled to England with a handsome pension, he bought the Georgian house in 1863 and commissioned John Norton to transform it into a palace modelled on those in Lahore and Delhi. Although it is stated that in private Duleep Singh referred to Queen Victoria as *"Mrs Fagin......receiver of stolen goods"* (the diamond), he kept close contact with the royal household and the Queen became his son's godmother. The Guinness family (Lord Iveagh) later took it over and joined in the fun, adding even more exotic adornments including a replica Taj Mahal, while at the same time creating the largest arable farm in the whole of the country.

Elveden and its purlieus, like so much of Suffolk, abounds in Neolithic and Iron Age sites, one of which was honoured with a visit by no less a person than Sir Arthur Evans, the British archaeologist who excavated the ruins of Knossos in Crete.

The Church of St Andrew and St Patrick dates in part from the 12th century; the oldest part was originally thatched, but the good Duleep Singh put on a slate roof. He is buried in the churchyard. To the south of the church is a bell tower put up in memory of Lady Iveagh and connected to the church by a cloister walk. Most of the other buildings in the village date from the end of the 19th century (the work of the Guinness family); the latest addition - outside the village - is the *Elveden Forest Holiday Village*.

Bury St Edmunds

A gem among Suffolk towns, rich in archaeological treasures and places of religious and historical interest. The town takes its name from St Edmund, who was born in Nuremberg in 841 and came here as a teenager to become the last king of East Anglia. He was a staunch Christian, and his refusal to deny his faith caused him to be tortured and killed by the Danes in 870. Legend has it that although his body was recovered, his head (cut off by the Danes) could not be found. His men searched for it for 40 days, then heard his voice directing them to it from the depths of a wood, where they discovered it lying protected between the paws of a wolf. The head and the body were seamlessly united and, to commemorate the wolf's deed, the crest of the town's armorial bearings depicts a wolf with a man's head.

Edmund was possibly buried first at Hoxne, the site of his murder, but when he was canonised in about 910 his remains were moved to the monastery at Beodricsworth, which changed its name to St Edmundsbury. A shrine was built in his honour, later incorporated into the Norman Abbey Church after the monastery was granted abbey status by King Canute in 1032. The town soon became a place of pilgrimage and for many years St Edmund was the patron saint of England, until replaced by St George. Growing rapidly around the great abbey, which became one of the largest and most influential in the land, Bury prospered as a centre of trade and commerce, thanks notably to the cloth industry.

The next historical landmark was reached in 1214, when on St Edmund's Feast Day the Archbishop of Canterbury, Simon Langton, met with the Barons of England at the high altar of the Abbey and swore that they would

Norman Tower, Bury St Edmunds Abbey

force King John to honour the proposals of the Magna Carta. The twin elements of Edmund's canonisation and the resolution of the Barons explain the motto on the town's crest: *"sacrarium regis, cunabula legis"* - *"shrine of a king, cradle of the law"*.
Rebuilt in the 15th century, the Abbey was largely dismantled after its dissolution by Henry VIII, but imposing ruins remain in the colourful Abbey Gardens beyond the splendid Abbey Gate and Norman Tower. **St Edmundsbury Cathedral** was originally the Church of St James, built in the 15th/16th century and accorded cathedral status (alone in Suffolk) in 1914. The original building has been much extended down the years (notably when being adapted for its role as a cathedral) and outstanding features include a magnificent hammerbeam roof, whose 38 beams are decorated with angels bearing the emblems of St James, St Edmund and St George. The monumental Bishop's throne depicts wolves guarding the crowned head of St Edmund, and there's a fascinating collection of 1,000 embroidered kneelers. Millennium funds granted in 1997 should guarantee that the tower which the cathedral lacks is finally built.

St Mary's Church, in the same complex, is also well worth a visit: an equally impressive hammerbeam roof, the detached tower standing much as Abbot Anselm built it in the 12th century, and several interesting monuments, the most important commemorating Mary Tudor, sister of Henry VIII, Queen of France and Duchess of Suffolk. Her remains were moved here when the Abbey was suppressed; a window in the Lady Chapel which records this fact was the gift of Queen Victoria.

The Abbey Visitor Centre, open daily from Easter to the end of October, is situated in Samson's Tower, part of the west front of the Abbey. The centre has displays and hands-on activities concerning the Abbey's history. **The Abbey Gardens**, which were laid out in 1831, have as their central feature a great circle of flower beds following the pattern of the Royal Botanical Gardens in Brussels. Some of the original ornamental trees can still be seen, and other - later - features include an Old English rose garden, a water garden and a garden for the blind where fragrance counts for all. Ducks and geese live by the little River Lark, and there are tennis courts, putting and bowls greens and children's play equipment.

Ash Cottage is a 16th century timbered town house a short walk up from the Abbey Gardens and close to many of Bury's other historic sites. Elizabeth Barber-Lomax's house is rich in old-world character, with many sturdy beams, and guests can choose between a double room with en suite facilities and a twin with private shower. These rooms overlook a wonderful cottage garden which annually (on a Sunday in June) is one of the many 'Hidden Gardens' open to the public on a day which raises funds for the St Nicholas Hospice - a cause well worth supporting on any day of the year. No smoking. *Ash Cottage, 59 Whiting Street, Bury St Edmunds, Suffolk, IP33 1NP. Tel: 01284 755098* Bury is full of fine non-ecclesiastical buildings, many with Georgian frontages concealing medieval interiors. Among the most interesting are

Ash Cottage

the handsome **Manor House Museum** with its collection of clocks, paintings, furniture, costumes and objets d'art; the **Victorian Corn Exchange** with its imposing colonnade; the Athenaeum, hub of social life since Regency times and scene of Charles Dickens's public readings; **Cupola House**, where Daniel Defoe once stayed; the **Angel Hotel**, where Dickens and his marvellous creation Mr Pickwick stayed; and the **Nutshell**, owned by Greene King Brewery and probably the smallest pub in the country. (Tours of the town's Greene King Brewery can be booked by calling 01284 763222.) **The Theatre Royal**, now in the care of the National Trust, was built in 1819 by William Wilkins, who was also responsible for the National Gallery. It once staged the premiere of *Charley's Aunt* and still operates as a working theatre.

In a Grade II listed building dating from 1825, **Mamma Roma** is a small, cosy Italian restaurant with a permanent party atmosphere. Leading the party is the flamboyant Roman owner Franco Mazzoccia, who has won fame (including television appearances) as

Mamma Roma

a singing chef. He makes his own pasta while serenading the customers with arias from the Italian classics, keeping everyone both happy and well fed. Italian classics also make up the menu, with specialities that include wild boar cooked in a Barolo wine sauce, osso buco and seasonal game and seafood. Much of the cooking is done in the original ovens of this one-time bakery, using the handsome long-handled implements of the period. Open Sunday lunch and Tuesday to Sunday dinner. *Mamma Roma, 28/29 Canon Street, Bury St Edmunds, Suffolk, IP33 1JR. Tel: 01284 754855*

The Bury St Edmunds Art Gallery is housed in one of Bury's noblest buildings, built to a Robert Adam design in 1774. It filled many roles down the years, and was rescued from decline in the 1960s to be restored to Adam's original plans. It is now one of the county's premier art galleries, with eight exhibitions each year and a thriving craft shop. The first exhibition, in 1972, was a particularly happy choice - *Two Hundred Years of Suffolk Art* included the work of Constable, Gainsborough and Munnings. The high quality of exhibitions, involving not just painting but the whole spectrum of artistic skills, has been maintained by a succession of gifted administrators (Barbara Taylor currently holds the post), and some exhibitions tour the country, publicising and enhancing the gallery's reputation.

In the last few years the gallery shop has proved a great success, and regular workshops and children's days enable the public to play

The Bury St Edmunds Art Gallery

an active role in the creative process. *Bury St Edmunds Art Gallery, The Market Cross, Bury St Edmunds, Suffolk, IP33 1BT. Tel: 01284 762081*

Perhaps the most fascinating building of all is **Moyses Hall** at one end of the Buttermarket. Built of flint and limestone about 1180, it has claims to being the oldest stone domestic building in England. Originally a rich man's residence, it later saw service as a prison, a workhouse, a police station and a railway office, and for the past 100 years it has been a museum. It houses some 10,000 items, from a Bronze Age hoard, Roman pottery and Anglo-Saxon jewellery to a 19th century doll's house and some grisly relics of the notorious Red Barn murder.

Outside the Spread Eagle pub on the western edge of town is a horse trough erected to the memory of the Victorian romantic novelist Ouida (Maria Louisa Ramee, 1839-1908).

39 Well Street is home to Sue Harrington-Spier and her cats and dogs. It's also a quiet, civilised home from home for paying guests,

39 Well Street

who will quickly feel like members of the family. The house is part of a well-preserved period terrace just off the centre and close to Bury's shops and places of historic interest. There are three comfortably appointed bedrooms, all with plenty of character and one with full en suite facilities; the ground-floor room boasts a fine Regency fireplace and opens on to the walled rose garden - a fine spot for summer breakfasts. Public areas comprise a large, antique-furnished hallway and a kitchen/dining room for guests. *39 Well Street, Bury St Edmunds, Suffolk, IP33 1EQ. Tel: 01284 768986*

Steeped though it is in history, Bury also moves with the times, and its sporting and leisure facilities are impressive. A mile and a half outside town on the A14 (just off the East Exit) is **Nowton Park**, 172 acres of countryside landscaped in Victorian style and supporting a wealth of flora and fauna; the avenue of limes, carpeted with daffodils in the spring, is a particular delight. There's also a play area and a ranger centre.

Bury is a wonderful place to visit, with almost 1,000 preserved buildings and a disciplined network of streets (the layout was devised in the 11th century) that provide long, alluring views. Locals protesting against the poll tax of their day did sporadic damage, but a great fire destroyed much of Bury in 1608; it was rebuilt using traditional timber-framing techniques. Arriving here in 1698 Celia Fiennes, the inveterate traveller and critic of architecture, remarked that *"there are no good houses but only what are old and rambling"* but she made an exception of Cupola House, which was just about completed at the time of her visit. William Cobbett (1763-1835), a visitor when chronicling his *Rural Rides*, did not disagree with the view that Bury St Edmunds was *"the nicest town in the world"* - a view which would be endorsed by many of its inhabitants and by many of the millions of visitors who have been charmed by this jewel in Suffolk's crown.

South Hill House, on the way into town from the A134, is part of the property once owned by the Gage family of Hengrave Hall (see under Hengrave). It became an academy for young ladies in the mid-1800s, when Charles Dickens came to give readings. Next it was a boarding school for boys, and the bell tower harks back to those days. In recent years Sarah Green's house has been winning high marks offering bed and breakfast accommodation in agreeably relaxed surroundings. There are three en suite bedrooms - a twin with shower, a double and a large family room. No smoking in the bedrooms. No pets. Off-street parking is available on the premises. *South Hill House, 43 Southgate Street, Bury St Edmunds, Suffolk, IP33 2AZ. Tel: 01284 755650*

South Hill House

Around Bury St Edmunds

Great and Little Saxham
Map 1 ref C5
3 miles W of Bury St Edmunds off the A14

St Andrew's Church in Great Saxham was restored in the 18th century and features a Stuart pulpit, a Perpendicular font and some magnificent stained glass. A brass dated 1632 commemorates one John Eldred, the man who first brought nutmeg to England. Having made a fortune from importing spices, he built himself a mansion called Nutmeg Hall - no longer in existence.

In Little Saxham, formerly Saxham Parva, the Norman flintstone Church of St Nicholas has a lovely round tower, a restored Jacobean pulpit, a Stuart bier with sliding handles and reclining animals carved into the bench ends.

Risby *Map 1 ref C5*
4 miles W of Bury St Edmunds off the A14

A farming village mentioned in the Domesday Book and once in the ownership of the Abbey of Bury St Edmunds. Two major attractions: a flint-walled church with a Saxon round tower, a beautifully restored 15th century rood screen and some even older wall paintings; and a major antiques centre in a medieval thatched barn.

Hengrave *Map 1 ref C5*
3 miles NW of Bury St Edmunds on the A1101

A captivating old-world village of flint and thatch. Excavations and aerial photography indicate that a settlement has been here since Neolithic times, and the parts of the village of archaeological interest are now protected. The chief attraction is **Hengrave Hall**, a rambling Tudor mansion built partly of Northamptonshire limestone and partly of yellow brick between 1525 and 1538 by Sir Thomas Kytson, a wool merchant. A notable visitor in the early days was Elizabeth I, who brought her court here in 1578. Several generations of the Gage family were later the owners and one of them, with a particular interest in horticulture, imported various kinds of plum tree from France. Most of the bundles were properly labelled with their names but one had lost its label. When it produced its first crop of luscious green fruit someone had the bright idea of calling it the green Gage. The name stuck, and the descendants of the trees, planted in 1724, are still at the Hall, which may be visited by appointment (Tel: 01284 701561). In the grounds stands a lovely little church with a round Saxon tower and a wealth of interesting monuments. The church was for some time a family mausoleum; restored by Sir John Wood, it became a private chapel and it now hosts services of various denominations.

Flempton *Map 1 ref C4*
4 miles NW of Bury St Edmunds on the A1101

An interesting walk from this village just north of the A1101 follows the **Lark Valley Park** through Culford Park, providing a good view of Culford Hall, which has been a school since 1935. A handsome cast-iron bridge dated from the early 19th century and recently brought to light from among the reeds crosses a lake in the park.

West Stow   *Map 1 ref C4*
4 miles NW of Bury St Edmunds off the A1101

The villages of West Stow, Culford, Ingham, Timworth and Wordwell were for several centuries part of a single estate covering almost 10,000 acres. Half the estate was sold to the Forestry Commission in 1935 and was renamed the King's Forest in honour of King George V's Jubilee in that year.

An Anglo-Saxon cemetery was discovered in the village in 1849 and the years since have revealed traces of Roman settlements and the actual layout of the original Anglo-Saxon village. A trust was established to investigate further the Anglo-Saxon way of life and their building and farming techniques. Several buildings were constructed using, as accurately as could be achieved, the tools and methods of the 5th century. The undertaking has become a major tourist attraction, with assistance from both human (in Anglo-Saxon costume) and cassette guides. There are pigs and hens and growing crops, craft courses, a Saxon market at Easter, a festival in August and special events all year round.

This fascinating village, which is entered through the Visitor Centre, is part of **West Stow Country Park**, a large part of which is designated a Site of Special Scientific Interest (SSSI). Over 120 species of bird and 25 species of animal have been sighted in this Breckland setting, and a well-marked 5-mile nature trail links this nature reserve with the woods, a large lake and the River Lark. Very near the park and village is Cow Wise, a working dairy farm with lots of animals for young visitors to feed.

Lackford   *Map 1 ref C4*
6 miles NW of Bury St Edmunds on the A1101

More interest here for the wildlife enthusiast. Restored gravel pits have been turned into a reserve for wildfowl and waders. Two hides are available.

Icklingham   *Map 1 ref B4*
8 miles NW of Bury St Edmunds on the A1101

Two churches in this village - the parish church of St James (mentioned in the Domesday Book) and the redundant thatched-roofed All Saints, with medieval tiles on the chancels and beautiful east windows in the south aisle. At the point where the Icknield Way crosses the River Lark, Icklingham has a long history, brought to light in frequent archaeological finds, from pagan bronzes to Roman coins. The place abounds in tales of the supernatural, notably of the white rabbit who is seen at dusk in the company of a witch, causing horses to bolt and men to die!

Just south of Icklingham, at the A1101, is **Rampart Field** picnic site, where pleasant walks through gorse-filled gravel workings reveal the varied plant life of a typical Breckland heath.

CHAPTER TWO
Southwest Suffolk

Suffolk Punch Horses

Chapter 2 - Area Covered

For precise location of places please refer to the colour maps found at the rear of the book.

2
Southwest Suffolk

Introduction

The area south and west of Bury towards the Essex border contains some of Suffolk's most attractive and peaceful countryside. The beauty is largely unspoilt and the motorist will come upon a succession of picturesque villages, historic churches, stately homes, heritage centres and nature reserves. In the south, along the River Stour, stand the historic wool towns of Long Melford, Cavendish and Clare.

There are some 500 medieval churches in Suffolk, each reflecting the life of its community and the changes effected by wars, invasions and religious upheavals. One of the most remarkable features of Suffolk churches is how long the sites have been occupied. 400 of those 500 sites were already consecrated by the time of the Norman invasion and the 500 survivors represent an impressively high percentage of the 550 or so thought to have been built.

Suffolk churches, many almost grand and dignified enough to be cathedrals, bear testimony to the prosperity, both personal and communal, of the 14th and 15th centuries, when the cloth and weaving industries made Suffolk one of the richest parts of the country. The resources were available, and so were the skills, notably those of the flint workers for the external walls, and the carpenters, for specialised work on rood screens and some often amazing roof structures, typically hammerbeams above a choir of angels. No less a critic than the art historian Kenneth Clark ('Lord Clark of Civilisation') asserted that *"Suffolk churches are (with the possible exception of the Wash churches) the most beautiful in England"*. Clark also knew that the motives behind the grandeur were not always selfless. A simple wish to outdo the rich man in the next village was no doubt a frequent reason for an ostentatious show of wealth, but equally certainly some of the building was done with more than a glance towards Heaven. As Clark says, *"Without the doctrine of Purgatory the number of fine buildings would have been substantially reduced, and without the fear of Hell they might not have existed at all"*.

Changes naturally took place down the years - stone towers built, porches or aisles added - and much restoration work was carried out in the Victorian period. A time of danger and disaster for the churches was from the Dissolution of the Monasteries under Henry VIII through to Cromwell, the Civil War and the Commonwealth. The Puritans regarded icons and ornaments as images of popery, works of idolatry standing between Man and God. This religious fervour led to systematic attacks on stained glass, paintings and sculptures, and the chief culprit in East Anglia was the serial iconoclast William Dowsing, a son of Laxfield. This person was employed by the Earl of Manchester, during the Commonwealth, for the *"defacing, demolishing and quite taking away of all images, altars ... crucifixes, superstitious pictures, monuments and reliques of idolatry, out of all churches and chapels"*. His orgy of destruction was recorded in great detail in his journal, and the damage caused by Dowsing and his cohorts removed much of the visual beauty and mystery from a large number of churches.

Natural causes and anno domini have also taken their toll, but the Suffolk church remains one of the county's greatest glories, and enough devoted citizens and charities are around to keep it that way.

Many of the churches described in this and other Chapters of the book are known almost the world over, while others stand off the beaten track in humble tranquillity, waiting to surprise and delight the visitor.

South of Bury St Edmunds

Great Welnetham   *Map 1 ref D6*
2 miles S of Bury St Edmunds off the A134
One of the many surviving Suffolk windmills is to be found here, just south of the village. The sails were lost in a gale 80 years ago but the tower and a neighbouring old barn make an attractive sight.

The Bradfields
7 miles SE of Bury St Edmunds off the A134

Map 2 ref D6

The Bradfields - St George, St Clare and Combust - and Cockfield thread their way through a delightful part of the countryside and are well worth a little exploration, not only to see the picturesque villages themselves but for a stroll in the historic **Bradfield Woods**. These woods stand on the eastern edge of the parish of Bradfield St George and have been turned into an outstanding nature reserve, tended and coppiced in the same way for more than 700 years and home to a wide variety of flora and fauna. They once belonged to the Abbey of St Edmundsbury and part of them is still today called Monk's Park Wood.

Coppicing involves cutting a tree back down to the ground every ten years or so. Woodlands were managed in this way to provide an annual crop of timber for local use, and the regrowth after coppicing is very fast as the root is already strongly established. Willow and hazel are the trees most commonly coppiced. Willow is often pollarded, a less drastic form of coppicing where the trees are cut far enough from the ground to stop grazing animals having a free lunch.

Long-time occupants and recent owners Bob and Mary Stimson offer a real taste of country house living in **Cargate House**, which enjoys a setting of enviable peace and tranquillity in a village 7 miles south east of Bury. In front of the house stands an ancient, imposing Wellingtonia tree, beyond which fields and woods open up miles of glorious views. The grounds include extensive lawns, a moat

Cargate House

stocked with golden orfe and rudd, and kitchen gardens that yield provisions all the year round. Accommodation comprises two en suite bedrooms (one with double bed, one with double and single) and a smaller single, and guests take breakfast in the dining room. The owners are happy to share their impressive knowledge of local history and wildlife. Horse-riding is available in the vicinity. *Cargate House, Bradfield St George, Near Bury St Edmunds, Suffolk, IP30 0AG. Tel: 01284 386698*

Bradfield St Clare, the central of the three Bradfields, has a rival claim to that of Hoxne as the site of the martyrdom of St Edmund. The St Clare family arrived with the Normans and added their name to the village, and the church, originally All Saints, was rededicated to St Clare; it is the only church in England dedicated to her. Bradfield Combust, where the pretty River Lark rises, probably takes it curious name from the fact that the local hall was burnt to the ground during the 14th century riots against the Abbot of St Edmundsbury's crippling tax demands. Arthur Young (1741-1820), noted writer on social, economic and agricultural subjects, is buried in the village churchyard.

Cockfield   Map 2 ref D6
8 miles SE of Bury St Edmunds off the A1141

Cockfield is perhaps the most widely spread village in all Suffolk, its little thatched cottages scattered around and between no fewer than nine greens. Great Green is the largest, with two football pitches and other recreation areas, and Parsonage Green has a literary connection: the **Old Rectory** was once home to a Dr Babbington, whose nephew Robert Louis Stephenson was a frequent visitor and who is said to have written *Treasure Island* while staying there. Cockfield also shelters one of the last windmills to have been built in Suffolk (1891). Its working life was very short but the tower still stands, now in use as a private residence.

In a village where everyone knows everyone and ducks take precedence over traffic, **Holly Cottage** is a sturdy brick-built house on the largest of several greens (Great Green). Edmund and Enid Golding keep two letting bedrooms, both very homely and cosy, one with the added character of bare brick walls.

Guests can relax in the garden among the myriad flowers and border plants, listening to the birds and enjoying the views. The westward vista from the rear is particularly attractive, with the rolling fields seeming to stretch out forever and Lawshall church in the distance. A good breakfast starts the day - English, Continental

Holly Cottage

or vegetarian. *Holly Cottage, Great Green, Cockfield, Near Bury St Edmunds, Suffolk, IP30 0HQ. Tel: 01284 828682*

Thorpe Morieux   Map 2 ref D7
9 miles SE of Bury St Edmunds off the B1071

St Mary's Church in Thorpe Morieux is situated in as pleasant a setting as anyone could wish to find. With water meadows, ponds, a stream and a fine Tudor farmhouse to set it off, this 14th century church presents a memorable picture of old England. Look at the church, then take the time to wander around the peaceful churchyard with its profusion of springtime aconites, followed by the colourful flowering of limes and chestnuts in the summer.

Marjorie Nicholls owns and runs **Mount Farm House**, a very special place for a civilised stay in a beautiful rural setting. Taste and quality are the watchwords throughout, and the residents' lounge and dining room, which open on to the gardens, are notable for their exquisite furnishings and fittings.

The three main-house bedrooms, each with its own character, show a similarly keen eye for design, with fetching colour coordination and handsome pieces of furniture; two rooms have brass bedsteads, the third a pine bed and matching fixtures. Three further bedrooms, with ground-floor accommodation and en suite facilities above, are in a beautiful converted barn, in whose entrance is a capacious sitting room and a breakfast room. Also in the extensive grounds which surround the property are an indoor swimming pool, a sauna and a tennis court.

Dinner can be arranged with advance notice and a residential licence for this purpose includes wines and spirits. Not a place for

Mount Farm House

families with young children, but a great choice for a honeymoon - or just a well-deserved treat! No smoking. *Mount Farm House, Thorpe Morieux, Suffolk, IP30 0NQ. Tel: 01787 248428*

Lawshall
Map 1 ref D6

8 miles S of Bury St Edmunds off the A134

A spread-out village first documented in 972 but regularly giving up evidence of earlier occupation. A Bronze Age sword dated at around 600BC was found here and is now in Bury Museum. The Church of All Saints, Perpendicular with some Early English bits, stands on one of the highest points in Suffolk, and next to it is Lawshall Hall whose owners once entertained Queen Elizabeth I. Another interesting site in Lawshall is the **Wishing Well**, a well-cover on the green put up in memory of Charles Tyrwhitt Drake, who worked for the Royal Geographic Society and was killed in Jerusalem.

Alpheton
Map 2 ref D7

10 miles S of Bury St Edmunds on the A134

Several points of interest at this little village straddling the main road. It was first settled in 991 and its name means the farm of *Aefflaed*. That lady was the wife of *Ealdorman Beorhtnoth* of Essex, who was killed resisting the Danes at the Battle of Maldon and is buried in Ely Minster.

The hall, the farm and the church stand in a quiet location away from the main road and about a mile from the village. This remoteness is not unusual: some attribute it to the villagers moving during times of plague but the more likely explanation is simply that the scattered cottages, originally in several tiny hamlets, centred, for whatever reason, in a more convenient site than that of the church. Equally possible is that it was built to suit the local landed family (that is to say, next door). The main features at the **Church of St Peter and St Paul** are the flintwork around the parapet (the exterior is otherwise fairly undistinguished), the carefully restored 15th century porch and some traces of an ancient wall painting of St Christopher with the Christ Child. All in all, a typical country church of unpretentious dignity and well worth a short detour from the busy main roads.

Back in the village, two oak trees were planted and a pump installed in 1887, to commemorate Queen Victoria's 50 years on the throne. The village's most recent claim to fame was when its American airfield was used as the setting for the classic film *Twelve o'Clock High*, in which Gregory Peck memorably plays a World War II flight commander cracking up under the strain of countless missions. Incidentally, one of the reasons for constructing the A134 was to help in the development of the airfield. The A134 continues south to Long Melford. An alternative road from Bury to Long Melford is the B1066, quieter and equally scenic, with a number of pleasant places to visit en route.

Whepstead   *Map 1 ref C6*
6 miles S of Bury St Edmunds on the B1066
Whepstead is a charming little village with three manor houses and a church dedicated to St Petronilla. Brockley Green, a village of some 300 souls, has a church that was built in the 13th and 14th centuries on a Saxon site. The tower dates from the 16th century and in the churchyard the base of a Tudor cross is to be seen.

Hartest   *Map 1 ref C7*
9 miles S of Bury St Edmunds on the B1066
Hartest, which has a history as long as Alpheton's, celebrated its millennium in 1990 with the erection of a village sign (the hart, or stag). It's an agreeable spot in a valley, with colour-washed houses and chestnut trees on the green. Also on the green are All Saints Church (mentioned in the Domesday Book) and a large glacial stone, *the Hartest stone*, which was dragged by a team of 45 horses from where it was found in a field in neighbouring Somerton. From 1789 until the 1930s Hartest staged a St George's Day Fair, an annual jolly celebrating King George III's recovery from one of his spells of madness. Just outside the village is **Gifford's Hall**, a smallholding which includes 12 acres of vines and a winery producing white and rosé wines and fruit liqueurs. There are also organic vegetable gar-

dens, wild flower meadows, black St Kilda sheep, black Berkshire pigs, goats and free-range fowl. The Hall is particularly famous for its sweet peas and roses, and an annual festival is held on the last weekend in June. Open from Easter to the end of October. Tel: 01284 830464.

Boxted
Map 1 ref C7

10 miles S of Bury St Edmunds on the B1066

The Church of the Holy Trinity has a private pew for the Poley family, who were clearly the top people of the village in their day. The pew is raised above the general level, which could be just to show their social superiority but also has other uses – keeping out damp, draughts and dogs are some!

Shimpling
Map 1 ref C7

9 miles S of Bury St Edmunds off the B1066

Shimpling is a peaceful farming community whose church, St George's, is approached by a lime avenue. It is notable for Victorian stained glass and a Norman font, and in the churchyard is the ***Faint House***, a small stone building where ladies overcome by the tightness of their stays could decently retreat from the service. The banker Thomas Hallifax built many of Shimpling's cottages and also the village school and Chadacre Hall, which Lord Iveagh later turned into an agricultural college (that role ceased in 1989 and the Hall is again in private hands).

In a peaceful setting of thatch and birdsong, ***The Bush*** is run by Joe and Sue Massey and their four sons. It's a thriving pub and very

The Bush

much the centre of village life. Built in 1750 as a farrier's yard, it changed its role when Shimpling split from Shimpling Street, leaving the former stranded without a pub. The outside is covered in ivy, while notable interior features include extensive floor tiling, old pew-style seating and a wealth of local history in the form of pictures, documents and stories from Sue. It's a place of wide appeal, equally popular with couples during the week and families at weekends. There's a huge enclosed garden with a pond and picnic tables, and the children's play area is set well away from the access lane.

Ducks, chickens, geese, rabbits and goats all add to the fun, while a little healthy competition is available at the dart board or on the boules strip. Real ales. Home-cooked food. Shimpling's church is well worth a visit for its fine Victorian stained glass and Norman font. *The Bush, Shimpling, Near Bury St Edmunds, Suffolk, IP29 4HU. Tel: 01284 828257*

Glemsford
Map 1 ref C7
12 miles S of Bury St Edmunds off the B1066
Driving in from the north on the B1066, the old Church of St Mary makes an impressive sight on what, for Suffolk, is a quite considerable hill. Textiles and weaving have long played a prominent part in Glemsford's history, and thread from the silk factory has been woven into dresses and robes for various members of the present royal family. During the last century several factories produced matting from coconut fibres and in 1906 Glemsford was responsible for the largest carpet in the world to cover the floor at London's Olympia. To this day one factory processes horse hair for use in judges' wigs, sporrans and busbies.

Long Melford
Map 1 ref D8
13 miles S of Bury St Edmunds off the A134
The heart of this atmospheric wool town is a very long and, in stretches, fairly broad main street, set on an ancient Roman site in a particularly beautiful part of south Suffolk. In Roman times the Stour was a navigable river and trade flourished. Various Roman finds have been unearthed, notably a blue glass vase which is now on display in the British Museum. The street is filled with antique shops, book shops and art galleries and is a favourite place for collectors and browsers. Some of the houses are washed in the characteristic Suffolk pink, which might originally have been achieved by mixing ox blood or sloe juice into the plaster.

Holy Trinity Church, on a 14-acre green at the north end of Hall Street, is a typical exuberant manifestation of the wealth of the wool and textile trade. It's big enough to be a cathedral, but served (and still serves) comparatively few parishioners. John Clopton, grown rich in the woollen business, was largely responsible for this magnificent Perpendicular-style edifice, which has a 180-foot nave and chancel and half timbers, flint flashwork of the highest quality and 100 large windows to give a marvellous sense of light and space. Medieval glass in the north aisle depicts religious scenes and the womenfolk of the Clopton family. There are many interesting monuments and brasses, and in the chantry entrance is a bas relief of the Three Wise Men, the Virgin and Child, and St Joseph. In the chantry proper are the altar, sedilia (seats for officiating priests), piscina (a basin for washing communion vessels) and niches once occupied by figures of the Apostles. In the Lady Chapel, reached by way of the churchyard, a children's multiplication table written on a wall is a reminder that the chapel served as the village school for a long period after the Reformation.

John Clopton's largesse is recorded rather modestly in inscriptions on the roof parapets. His tower was struck by lightning in the early 18th century and the present brick construction dates from around 1900. The detail of this great church is of endless fascination, but it's the overall impression that stays in the memory, and the sight of the building floodlit at night is truly spectacular. The distinguished 20th century poet Edmund Blunden spent his last years in Long Melford and is buried in the churchyard. The inscription on his gravestone reads *"I live still to love still things quiet and unconcerned"*.

Melford Hall, east of town beyond an imposing 16th gateway, was built around 1570 by Sir William Cordell on the site of an earlier hall that served as a country retreat, before the Dissolution of the Monasteries, for the monks of St Edmundsbury Abbey. There exists an account of Cordell entertaining Queen Elizabeth I at the Hall in 1578, when she was welcomed by *"200 young gentlemen in white velvet, 300 in black and 1,500 serving men"*. Much of the fine work of Sir William (whose body lies in Holy Trinity Church) has been altered in restoration, but the pepperpot chimneys are original, as is the panelled banqueting hall. The rooms are in various styles, some with ornate walnut furniture, and there's a notable collection of Chinese porcelain on show. Most delightful of all is the Beatrix Potter room, with some of her water colours, first editions of books and, among the toys, the original of Jemima Puddleduck. She was a frequent visitor here (her cousins the Hyde Parkers were the owners), bringing small animals to draw. The Jeremy Fisher illustrations were mostly drawn at Melford Hall's fishponds, and the book is dedicated to Stephanie Hyde Parker. The Parkers were a very prominent family. Admiral Sir Hyde Parker sailed around the world with Lord Anson and commanded the North Sea Fleet in 1781 at the Battle of Dogger Bank against the Dutch. His son, also Hyde Parker, is the man to whom Nelson turned a blind eye at Copenhagen when the order to stop the action was given. The Hall, which is a National Trust property, stands in a lovely garden with some distinguished clipped box hedges. William Cordell was also responsible for the red-brick almshouses, built in 1593 for '12 poor men', which stand near Holy Trinity.

Kentwell Hall is a red-brick Tudor moated mansion approached by a long avenue of limes. Its grounds include a unique Tudor rose maze. It sets out to illustrate and recreate Tudor times, with a walled garden, a bakery, a dairy and several varieties of rare-breed farm animals. The buildings include a handsome 14th century aisle barn. The Hall was the setting for the recent film version of *Toad of Toad Hall*.

Long Melford is a great place for leisurely strolls, and for the slightly more energetic there's a scenic 3-mile walk along a disused railway track and farm tracks that lead straight into Lavenham and Chapter 6 (the less energetic may tarry in Chapter 2).

Cavendish   Map 1 ref C7
3 miles W of Long Melford on the A1092

A most attractive village, where the Romans stayed awhile - the odd remains have been unearthed - and the Saxons settled. The

The Green, Cavendish

look is splendidly traditional, with the church, thatched cottages, almshouses, Nether Hall and the **Sue Ryder Foundation Museum** spread around the green. The last, in a 16th century rectory by the pond, illustrates the work of the Sue Ryder Foundation, and was formally opened by Queen Elizabeth in 1979. Once a refuge for concentration camp victims, it houses abundant war photographs and memorabilia. Nether Hall is a well-restored 16th century building and the headquarters of **Cavendish Vineyards**.

In the **Church of St Mary**, whose tower has a pointed bellcote and a room inside complete with fireplace and shuttered windows, look for the two handsome lecterns, one with a brass eagle (15th century), the other with two chained books; and for the Flemish and Italian statues. In 1381 Wat Tyler, leader of the Peasants revolt, was killed at Smithfield, in London, by John Cavendish, son of Sir John Cavendish, lord of the manor and Chief Justice of England. Sir John was hounded by the peasants, who caught him and killed him near Bury St Edmunds. He managed en route to hide some valuables in the belfry of St Mary's, Cavendish, and bequeathed to the church £40, sufficient to restore the chancel. A later Cavendish – Thomas – sailed round the world in the 1580s and perished on a second voyage. In the shadow of the church, on the edge of the village green, is a cluster of immaculate thatched cottages at a spot known as Hyde Park Corner. Pink-washed and pretty as a picture, they look almost too good to be true – and they almost are, having been rebuilt twice since World War II due to a combination of fire and dilapidation.

Clare   Map 1 ref B8
6 miles W of Long Melford on the A1092

A medieval wool town of great importance, Clare repays a visit today with its fine old buildings and some old ruins. Perhaps the most renowned tourist attraction is **Ancient House**, a timber-framed building dated 1473 and remarkable for its *pargeting*. This is the decorative treatment of external plasterwork, usually by dividing the surface into rectangles and decorating each panel. It was very much a Suffolk speciality, particularly in the 16th and 17th centuries, with some examples also being found in Cambridgeshire and Essex. The decoration could be simple brushes of a comb, scrolls or squiggles, or more elaborate, with religious motifs, guild signs or family crests. Some pargeting is incised, but the best is in relief – pressing moulds into wet plaster or shaping by hand. Ancient House sports some splendid twining flowers and branches, and a repre-

The Ancient House

sentation of two figures holding a shield. The best-known workers in this unique skill had their own distinctive styles, and the expert eye could spot the particular 'trademarks' of each man (the same is the case with the master thatchers). Ancient House is now a museum, open during the summer months with an exhibition of local history.

Another place of historical significance is **Nethergate House**, once the work place of dyers, weavers and spinners. The Swan Inn, in the High Street, has a sign which lays claim to being the oldest in the land. Ten feet in length and carved from a solid piece of wood, it portrays the arms of England and France.

The Church of St Peter and St Paul dates from the 13th century and stands on the site of an earlier (Saxon) church. Notable for its feeling of light and space, it features a brick-lined tower, superb carvings on Jacobean choir stalls and a 16th century Flemish eagle lectern which doubles as a box for donations.

Clare Castle was a motte and bailey fortress that sheltered a household of 250. **Clare Castle Country Park**, with a visitor centre in the goods shed of a disused railway line, contains the remains of the castle and the moat, the latter now a series of ponds and home to varied wild life. At the Prior's House, the original cellar and infirmary are still in use. Established in 1248 by Augustine friars and used by them until the Dissolution of 1538, the priory was handed back to that order in 1953 and remains their property.

A friendly welcome from Jean and Alastair Tuffill awaits you at **Cobwebs**. Situated in one of the loveliest parts of East Anglia, Cobwebs is a delightful, Listed 14th century beamed house. It is within easy walking distance of the historic town centre, including antique shops, the delightful castle ruins and the country park, and good pubs and restaurants for evening meals. Within the house there is one single and one twin-bedded bedroom. In the pretty walled garden, complete with rockery and water garden, is a separate twin-bedded en suite cottage with its own sitting area and private access. All rooms have central heating, colour TV, handbasins

Cobwebs

and tea/coffee making facilities. Cobwebs is a no-smoking establishment. *Cobwebs, 26 Nethergate Street, Clare, Suffolk, CO10 8NP. Tel: 01787 277539 Fax: 01787 278252*

A mile or so west of Clare on the A1092 lies **Stoke-by-Clare**, a pretty village on one of the region's most picturesque routes. It once housed a Benedictine priory, whose remains are now in the grounds of a school. There's a fine 15th century church and a vineyard: **Boyton Vineyards** at Hill Farm, Boyton End, is open early April-end October for a tour, a talk and a taste.

Haverhill

Map 1 ref A8

12 miles W of Long Melford on the A604

Notable for its fine Victorian architecture. Fire destroyed many of the town's buildings in 1665, but **Anne of Cleves House** was restored and is well worth a visit. Anne was the fourth wife of Henry VIII and after a brief political marriage she was given an allowance and spent the remainder of her days at Haverhill and Richmond. **East Town Park** is a new country park on the east side of Haverhill.

Around Haverhill

Kedington

Map 1 ref B7

2 miles N of Haverhill on the B1061

Haverhill intrudes somewhat, but the heart of the old village gains in appeal from the presence of the River Stour. Known to many as the *'Cathedral of West Suffolk'*, the **Church of St Peter and St Paul** is the chief attraction of Kedington. Almost 150' in length, it stands on a ridge overlooking the Stour Valley. It has several interesting features, including a 15th century font, a Saxon cross in the chancel window, a three-decker pulpit (with a clerk's desk and a reading desk) and a sermon-timer, looking rather like a grand eggtimer. The foundations of a Roman building have been found beneath the floorboards.

The Bardiston family, one of the oldest in Suffolk, has strong links with the village and many of the family tombs are in the church. In the church grounds is a row of ten elm trees, each, the legend says, with a knight buried beneath its roots.

Following the Stour along the B1061, the visitor will find a number of interesting little villages. In Little Wratting, Holy Trinity Church has a shingled oak-framed steeple (a feature more usually associated with Essex churches). John Sainsbury was a local resident, while in Great Wratting another magnate, W H Smith, financed the restoration of St Mary's Church in 1887. This church boasts some diverting topiary in the shape of a church, a cross and an armchair.

Great and Little Thurlow

Map 1 ref A7

3 miles N of Haverhill on the B1061

Great and Little Thurlow form a continuous village on the west bank of the Stour four miles north of Haverhill. Largely undamaged thanks to being in a conservation area, they have many 17th century cottages and a Georgian manor house. In the main street is a schoolhouse built in 1614 by Sir Stephen Soame, sometime Lord Mayor of London, whose family are commemorated in the village church.

A short distance further up the B1061 stands the village of **Great Bradley**, divided in two by the River Stour, which rises just outside the village boundary. Chief points of note in the tranquil parish church are a fine Norman doorway sheltering a Tudor brick porch and some beautiful stained glass poignantly depicting a soldier in the trenches during the First World War. The three bells in the tower include one cast in the 14th century, one of the oldest in Suffolk.

Denston   Map 1 ref B7
6 miles NE of Haverhill just off the A143
Denston lies just east of the A143 on the River Glem and is notable chiefly for its magnificent Perpendicular church, one of 18 dedicated to St Nicholas, patron saint of sailors. Stop and admire the fan vaulting in the roof (a comparative rarity in Suffolk), the outstanding brasses and the wide variety of carved animals.

Also on the Glem is the neighbouring village of Stansfield, where stand the ruins of another mill, this one a tower mill but without its cap and in a sorry state.

Hawkedon   Map 1 ref C7
7 miles NE of Haverhill off the A143
On to Hawkedon, designated a place of outstanding beauty, where the Church of St Mary is located untypically in the middle of the village green. The pews and intricately carved bench-ends take the eye here, along with a canopied stoup (a recess for holding holy water) and a Norman font. There is a wide variety of carved animals, many on the bench-ends but some on the roof cornice. One of the stalls is decorated with the carving of a crane holding a stone in its claw; legend says that if it was on watch and fell asleep, the stone would drop and the noise would wake it.

Hawkedon Pew

Wickhambrook
Map 1 ref B6

8 miles NE of Haverhill on the B1063

Wickhambrook is a series of tiny hamlets with no fewer than 11 greens and three manor houses. The greens have unusual names - Genesis, Nunnery, Meeting, Coltsfoot - whose origins keep local historians busy.

One of the two pubs has a split personality, being officially half in Wickhambrook and half in Denston.

Chedburgh
Map 1 ref C6

11 miles NE of Haverhill on the A143

Farm parks are an excellent way of discovering the county's rural and agricultural legacy and **Rede Hall Farm Park**, near Chedburgh, is modelled on a working farm of the 1930-1950 period. The Suffolk Punch can be seen at work here, and there are rare breeds of farm animals, a nature trail, cart rides and working displays. Also picnic and play areas, a tea room and a gift shop. Open April-September. Tel: 01284 850695.

Suffolk Punch Horses

Horringer   Map 1 ref C5
3 miles SW of Bury St Edmunds on the A143

Rejoining the A143 by Chedburgh, the motorist will soon arrive at Horringer, whose village green is dominated by the flintstone Church of St Leonard. Beside the church are the gates of one of the country's most extraordinary and fascinating houses, now run by the National Trust. *Ickworth House* was the brainchild of the eccentric 4th Earl of Bristol and Bishop of Derry, a collector of art treasures and an inveterate traveller (witness the Bristol Hotels scattered around Europe). His inspiration was Belle Isle, a house built on an island in Lake Windermere, and the massive structure is a central rotunda linking two semi-circular wings. It was designed as a treasure house for the arts and work started in 1795; the first collection of the Earl's treasures was seized by Napoleon in 1798 so never reached England.

Derry died in 1803 and his son, after some hesitation, saw the work through to completion in 1829. Its chief glories are some marvellous paintings by Titian, Gainsborough, Hogarth, Velasquez, Reynolds and Kauffman, but there's a great deal more to enthral the visitor: late Regency and 18th century French furniture, a notable collection of Georgian silver, friezes and sculptures by John Flaxman, frescoes copied from wall paintings discovered at the Villa Negroni in Rome in 1777. The Italian garden, where Mediterranean species have been bred to withstand a distinctly non-Mediterranean climate, should not be missed, with its hidden glades, orangery and temple rose garden, and in the Capability Brown park are designated walks and cycle routes, bird hides, a deer enclosure and play areas. The latest attractions are a vineyard and plant centre. The House is open Easter-end October, the park and gardens throughout the year. Tel: 01284 735270.

Arable land surrounds Horringer, with a large annual crop of sugar beet grown for processing at the factory in Bury, the largest of its kind in Europe.

CHAPTER THREE
Mid Suffolk

High Street, Debenham

Chapter 3 - Area Covered

For precise location of places please refer to the colour maps found at the rear of the book.

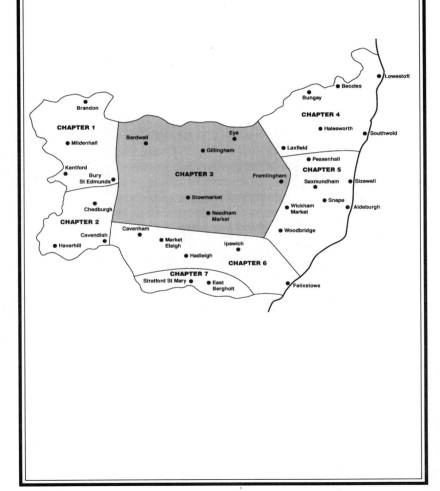

3
Mid Suffolk

Introduction

The heart of Suffolk, *the* place in the county to get away from it all, lying between the heathland and the coast. Many of the villages are little changed from olden days, the poppies put on a colourful show in the hedgerows, the pubs always offer a warm welcome and there are plenty of places to pause for the night, whether you want a hotel, an inn, a family-run B&B or a camping/caravan park. The Rivers Deben and Gipping run through much of the region, which naturally has its fair share of churches, museums, fayres and festivals. The little market towns of Stowmarket and Needham Market are full of interest and in this part of Suffolk some of the best-preserved windmills and watermills are to be found.

Windmills have been part of the Suffolk scene for 800 years, and William Cobbett, writing in 1830, spoke of seeing 17 from a single vantage point. 200 windmills were working in Suffolk at the turn of the century, hardly a dozen by the outbreak of World War II. Today in Suffolk about 20 windmills and the same number of watermills survive in more or less working order, most of them preserved and maintained at considerable cost by government or local subscriptions. The earliest windmills were post mills, in which the whole body - sails, mechanism and all - could be turned to face the wind on a huge central oak post. The end of the 18th century saw the introduction of tower mills, in which the machinery was contained in a fixed brick tower and only the cap with the sails could move to face into the wind. Tower mills with frames made of timber rather than brick were known as *smock mills*. Watermills were powered of course by the force of moving water, and since Suffolk is a fairly flat county some mills replaced the waterwheel with a much more efficient turbine. Several examples of both windmills and watermills survive in Suffolk, and Pakenham is lucky in having a splendid example of each.

North and East of Bury St Edmunds

Great Barton
Map 2 ref D5

2 miles NE of Bury St Edmunds on the A143

A scattered village that began life as a Saxon settlement and later assumed an important role as the granary and ice store for the Abbey at Bury. Sir Charles Bunbury, whom we have already met, once lived at Barton Hall. The Hall no longer exists, but the legacy of the philanthropic Bunbury family survives in the village school and almshouses. The Church of the Holy Innocents sports the Suffolk trademark hammerbeam roof and carved angels, but only one of the angels survived the Cromwellian onslaught.

Pakenham
Map 2 ref D5

4 mile NE of Bury St Edmunds off the A143

On a side road just off the A143 (turn right just north of Great Barton), lies the village of Pakenham, whose long history has been unearthed in the shape of a Bronze Age barrow and kiln, and another kiln from Roman times.

Elsewhere in Pakenham are the 17th century **Nether Hall**, from whose lake in the park the village stream flows through the fen into the millpond, and from the same period **Newe House**, a handsome Jacobean building with Dutch gables and a two-storey porch. The Church of St Mary has an impressive carved Perpendicular font and in its adjacent vicarage is the famous Whistler Window - a painting by Rex Whistler of an 18th century parish priest. The fens were an important source of reeds, and many of Pakenham's buildings show off the thatcher's art.

Pakenham's current unique claim to fame is in being the only parish in England with a windmill *and* a watermill, both in working order. The **watermill** was built around 1814 on a site mentioned in the Domesday Book (the Roman excavations suggest that there could have been a mill here as far back as the 1st century AD). The mill, which is fed from Pakenham fen, has many interesting features, including the Blackstone oil engine, dating from around 1900, and the Tattersall Midget rollermill from 1913, a brave but not successful attempt to compete with the larger roller mills in the production of flour. The mill and the neighbouring recreation park are well worth a visit. Tel: 01787 247179.

No less remarkable is the **windmill**, one of the most famous in Suffolk. The black-tarred tower was built in 1831 and was in regular use until the 1950s. One of the best preserved mills in the county, she survived a lightning strike in 1971.

Thurston
Map 2 ref D5
4 miles E of Bury St Edmunds off the A14

The Grange Hotel is a handsome Tudor-style country house standing in lovely countryside four miles from Bury St Edmunds. Secluded in its own attractive gardens, it is the perfect setting for getting away from it all, or an ideal base for touring. The area has its share of picturesque villages and, for extended trips, the far-reaching A14

The Grange Hotel

is only a couple of miles away. The 13 bedrooms, individually decorated and with the usual modern comforts, range from a single with WC only to superior doubles, and a family room with a double and a single bed. The lounge bar opens on to a terrace and garden, and at mealtimes guests can choose between the Garden Restaurant and the more formal Adam Room, where à la carte lunches and dinners are served, with a traditional roast on Sunday. *The Grange Hotel, Barton Road, Thurston, Near Bury St Edmunds, Suffolk, IP31 3PQ. Tel: 01359 231260*

Ixworth
Map 2 ref D4

5 miles NE of Bury St Edmunds on the A143

One of the Iceni tribe's major settlements, with important Roman connections and, in the 12th century, the site of an Augustinian priory. The remains of the priory were incorporated into a Georgian house known as Ixworth Abbey, which stands among trees by the River Blackbourne. The village has many 14th century timber-framed dwellings, and the Church of St Mary dates from the same period, though with many later additions.

A stroll among Ixworth's ancient timber-framed buildings or a trek in the countryside will set up a thirst and appetite which can both be satisfied at *The Pykkerell*. Ron and Anna Goulding are the tenants at this 15th century coaching inn, where the old court house and various medieval barns are ranged around a patio/courtyard; the coaching entrance survives, complete with gates. The inn itself is rich in period character, with original carved ceilings, panelled walls, scrubbed wooden floors and church pew seating. Each separate area (fishermen's bar, locals' bar, lounge, library) has a unique, individual appeal, and huge log-burning fires keep the cold at bay. One of the most striking features is a collection of armour and weaponry in the library. At the back of the inn, the restaurant is as appealing as the rest of the place, a

The Pykkerell

beautiful setting for enjoying a leisurely meal from a menu that's supplemented by daily blackboard specials. The inn takes daily delivery of fresh local produce, the only frozen item in the kitchen being the ice cream! A unique offering is the Pierrade stone meal, with customers cooking their own selection of meat or fish on hot Alpine stones by their table. A well-annotated wine list tours the world. *The Pykkerell, High Street, Ixworth, Suffolk, IP31 2HH. Tel & Fax: 01359 230398*

A walk along Ixworth's main street provides plenty to interest visitors, nowhere more than *Ixworth Antiques*, whose premises were formerly the Guildhall. Resident owners Michael and Angela Ginders keep a varied, ever-changing stock that includes anything from small items of furniture to tableware, antique lighting and brassware, tea caddies and writing boxes. They regularly supply goods to Europe and the USA and can arrange shipping and delivery for items large and small. Hours are 10am-5pm (closed Saturday after 1pm and all Wednesday). *Ixworth Antiques, 17 High Street, Ixworth, Near Bury St Edmunds, Suffolk, IP31 2HH. Tel: 01359 231691*

A little way north of the village, on the A1088, are a nature trail and bird reserve at Ixworth Thorpe Farm. Tel: 01359 269444/269386. At this point a brief diversion northwards up the A1088 is very worth while.

Bardwell   *Map 2 ref E4*
7 miles NE of Bury St Edmunds just off the A1088
Here's another tower windmill. This one dates from the 1820s and was worked by wind for 100 years, then by an oil engine until 1941. It was restored in the 1980s, only to suffer severe damage in the great storm of October 1987, when its sails were torn off. Stoneground flour is still produced by an auxiliary engine, and there's an on-site bakery. Also in this delightful village are a 16th century inn and the Church of St Peter and St Paul, known particularly for its medieval stained glass.

Honington   *Map 2 ref D4*
7 miles NE of Bury St Edmunds on the A1088
Back on the A1088, the little village of Honington is the birthplace of the pastoral poet Robert Bloomfield (1766-1823), whose best known work is *The Farmer's Boy*. The house where he was born is now divided, one part called Bloomfield Cottage, the other Bloomfield Farmhouse. A brass plaque to his memory can be seen in All Saints Church, in whose graveyard his parents are buried.

Euston   *Map 2 ref D3*
9 miles N of Bury St Edmunds on the A1088
Euston Hall, on the A1088, has been the seat of the Dukes of Grafton for 300 years. It's open to the public on Thursday afternoons and is well worth a visit, not least for its portraits of Charles II and its paintings by Van Dyck, Lely and Stubbs. In the colourful landscaped grounds, the distinguished work of John Evelyn and William Kent, is an ice house disguised as an Italianate temple.

Euston's church, in the grounds of the Hall, is the only one in the county dedicated to St Genevieve. It's also one of only two Classical designs in the county, being rebuilt in 1676 on part of the original structure. The interior is richly decorated, with beautiful carving on the hexagonal pulpit, panelling around the walls and a carved panel of the Last Supper. Parts of this lovely wood carving are attributed by some to Grinling Gibbons. Behind the family pew is a marble memorial to Lord Arlington, who built the church.

Barnham
Map 2 ref D3

8 miles N of Bury St Edmunds off the A1088

On an arable 1,000-acre farm near the border with Norfolk, the heart of *East Farm* is a sturdy house with grey flint facing and shuttered upper windows. For bed and breakfast guests Margaret Heading offers two en suite bedrooms - one double, one twin - and a large lounge/dining room with TV. The garden and tracks through the

East Farm

farmland are at hand for a quiet stroll, but the area beckons with more serious options for the energetic visitor, notably rambles in the nearby extensive forests or hikes along Peddars Way and the National Trail. West Stow country park and Anglo-Saxon village (see Chapter 1) is a short drive away. No smoking in the bedrooms. *East Farm, Barnham, Near Thetford, Norfolk, IP24 2PB. Tel: 01842 890231*

Stanton
Map 2 ref E4

7 miles NE of Bury St Edmunds on the A143

Stanton was mentioned in the Domesday Book and the Romans were here before that. A double ration of medieval churches - All Saints and St John the Baptist - will satisfy the ecclesiastical scholar, while for more worldly indulgences **Wyken Vineyards** (Tel: 01359 250287) will have a strong appeal. Four acres of gardens - herb, knot, rose, kitchen and woodland - are on the same site, and the complex also includes an Elizabethan manor house, a 16th century barn, a country shop and a café. There's also a splendid woodland walk.

Barningham
Map 2 ref E3

8 miles NE of Bury St Edmunds on the B1111

Near the Norfolk border, Barningham was the first home of the firm of Fisons, which started in the late 18th century. Starting with a couple of windmills, they later installed one of the earliest steam mills in existence. The engine saw service for nearly 100 years and is now in an American museum; the mill building exists to this day, supplying animal feed.

This is marvellous walking country, and **Knettishall Heath Country Park**, on 400 acres of prime Breckland terrain, is the official starting place of the Peddars Way National Trail and of a path that stretches 77 miles to Great Yarmouth by way of the Little Ouse and Waveney valleys.

Walsham-le-Willows
Map 2 ref E4

9 miles NE of Bury St Edmunds off the A143

A pretty name for a pretty village, with weatherboarded and timber-framed cottages along the willow-banked river which flows throughout its length. **St Mary's Church** is no less pleasing to the eye, with its sturdy western tower and handsome windows in the Perpendicular style. Of particular interest inside is the superb tie and hammerbeam roof of the nave, and (unique in Suffolk and very rare elsewhere) a tiny circular medallion which hangs suspended from the nave wall, known as a *'Maiden's Garland'* or *'Virgin's Crant'*. These marked the pew seats of unmarried girls who had passed away, and the old custom was for the young men of the village to hang garlands of flowers from them on the anniversary of the girl's death. This particular example celebrates the virginity of one Mary Boyce, who died (so the inscription says) of a broken heart in 1685, just 20 years old. There is also a carving on the rood screen which looks rather like the face of a wolf: this may well be a reference to the benevolent creature that plays such an important role in the legend of St Edmund. A museum by the church has changing exhibitions of local history.

Ricklinghall   *Map 2 ref F4*
12 miles NE of BurySt Edmunds on the A143

More timber-framed buildings, some thatched, along the streets of the two villages, Superior and Inferior, which follow an underground stream running right through them. Each has a church dedicated to St Mary and featuring fine flintwork and tracery. The upper church, now closed, was used as a school for London evacuees during the Second World War.

Redgrave   *Map 2 ref F3*
13 miles NE of Bury St Edmunds on the B1113

Arachnophobes beware! Redgrave and Lopham Fens form a 360-acre reserve of reed and sedge beds where one of the most interesting inhabitants is the Great Raft Spider. The village is the source of the Little Ouse and Waveney rivers, which rise on either side of the B1113 and set off on their seaward journeys in opposite directions.

Thelnetham   *Map 2 ref E3*
12 miles NE of Bury St Edmunds off the B111

West of Redgrave, between the B1113 and the B1111, lies Thelnetham – another village, another windmill. This one, a tower mill, was built in 1819 to replace a post mill on the same site, and worked for 100 years. It has been lovingly restored. Stoneground flour is produced and sold at the mill. If you wish to visit you should set sail on a summer Sunday. Tel: 01473 726996.

Cotton   *Map 2 ref F5*
16 miles E of Bury St Edmunds off the B1113

South of Finningham, where Yew Tree House displays some fine pargeting, and just by Bacton, a lovely village originally built round seven greens, lies the village of Cotton, which should be visited for two reasons. One is to see the splendid 14th century flint Church of St Andrew, impressive in its dimensions and notable for its double hammerbeam roof with carved angels. The other is to pause awhile at the **Mechanical Music Museum**, open from June to September, where you will discover organs, street pianos, musical boxes, musical dolls, polyphons and a Wurlitzer theatre organ in a mock-up of a cinema.

Bury St Edmunds to Stowmarket

The direct route between Bury and Stowmarket is the busy A14, on or near which are several places of interest.

Hessett
Map 2 ref D5
4 miles E of Bury St Edmunds off the A14
Dedicated to St Ethelbert, King of East Anglia, Hessett's church has many remarkable features, particularly some beautiful 16th century glass and wall paintings, both of which somehow escaped the Puritan wave of destruction. Ethelbert was unlucky enough to get on the wrong side of the mighty Offa, King of the Mercians, and was killed by him at Hereford, in 794.

Woolpit
Map 2 ref E5
6 miles E of Bury St Edmunds on the A14
The Church of St Mary the Virgin is Woolpit's crowning glory, with a marvellous porch and one of the most magnificent double hammerbeam roofs. The village was long famous for its brick industry, and the majority of the old buildings are faced with *'Woolpit Whites'*. The yellowish-white brick looked very much like more expensive stone and for several centuries was widely exported. Some was used in the building of the Senate wing of the Capitol in Washington DC. Red bricks were also produced, and the **Bygones Museum** (open weekends in summer, Tel: 01359 240822) has a brick-making display and also tells the story of the evolution of the village.

Village Pump, Woolpit

Nearby is a moated site known as **Lady's Well**, a place of pilgrimage in the Middle Ages. The water from the spring was reputed to have healing properties, most efficacious in curing eye troubles.

A favourite Woolpit legend concerns the *Green Children*, a brother and sister with green complexions who appeared one day in a field, apparently attracted by church bells. Though hungry, they would eat nothing until some green beans were produced. Given shelter by the lord of the manor, they learned to speak English and said that they came from a place called St Martin. The boy survived for only a short time, but the girl thrived, lost her green colour, was baptised and married a man from King's Lynn – no doubt leaving many a Suffolk man green with envy!

A former public house dating from around 1600 provides the spacious premises for **John Heather Antiques**, run by John and his wife Ann. Their usual stock majors on Georgian and early 19th century furniture, much of it mahogany, and their expertise includes the restoration of period pieces and the manufacture of copies to order. They also stock items such as brassware and glass, and their customers come from all walks of life, making purchases large and small - the famous green children would probably have chosen a little brass bell. *John Heather Antiques, Old Crown, The Street, Woolpit, Near Bury St Edmunds, Suffolk, IP30 9SA. Tel: 01359 240297*

Elmswell
Map 2 ref E5
7 miles E of Bury St Edmunds off the A14
Clearly visible from the A14, the impressive Church of St John the Baptist with its massive flint tower stands at the entrance to the village facing Woolpit across the valley. A short drive north of Elmswell lies **Great Ashfield**, an unspoilt village whose now disused airfield played key roles in both World Wars. In the churchyard of the 13th century All Saints is a memorial to the Americans who died during World War II and inside is a commemorative altar. Some accounts say that Edmund was buried here in 903 after dying at the hands of the Danes; a cross was put up in his memory. The cross was replaced in the 19th century and now stands in the garden of Ashfield House.

Haughley
Map 2 ref F5
12 miles E of Bury St Edmunds off the A14
On the run into Stowmarket, Haughley once had the largest motte and bailey castle in Suffolk. All that now remains is a mound behind the church. **Haughley Park** is a handsome redbrick mansion

set in eight acres of gardens and surrounding woodland featuring ancient oaks and splendid magnolias. Woodland paths take you past a half-mile stretch of rhododendrons, and in springtime the bluebells and lilies of the valley are a magical sight. The gardens are open on Tuesdays between May and September, the house by appointment only. Tel: 01359 240205.

Overlooking the green of a quaint village with some pretty thatched cottages, *The Old Counting House Restaurant* is a medieval (1360) timber-framed building whose name identifies its original purpose. Paul and Sue Woods came here in the early 1980s and haven't looked back, welcoming visitors into a cosy and relaxed setting of low ceilings and exposed beams.

The Old Counting House Restaurant

The fixed-price menus (2 or 3 courses for lunch, 4 courses in the evening) change every three weeks, and there are always vegetarian main courses as well as a choice of fish and meat dishes of English and French inspiration; children's meals and portions can be arranged. An extensive wine list complements the fine cooking. Lighter meals are available lunchtime and evening in the bar, which is also open to non-diners. Outside, the colourful flower display has earned the restaurant prizes in the 'Anglia in Bloom' competition. Closed lunchtime Saturday and all Sunday. *The Old Counting House Restaurant, Haughley, Near Stowmarket, Suffolk, IP14 3NR. Tel: 01449 673617*

Harleston

Map 2 ref E6

9 miles E of Bury St Edmunds off the A14

The churches of Shelland and Harleston lie in close proximity on a minor road between Woolpit and Haughley picnic site. At Shelland, the tiny Church of King Charles the Martyr is one of only four in England to be dedicated to King Charles I. The brick floor is laid in a herringbone pattern, there are high box pews and a three-decker pulpit, but the most unusual accessory is a working barrel organ dating from the early 19th century.

The Church of St Augustine at Harleston stands all alone among pine trees and is reached by a track across a field. It has a thatched roof, Early English windows and a tower with a single bell.

Stowmarket

The largest town in the heart of Suffolk, Stowmarket enjoyed a period of rapid growth when the River Gipping was still navigable to Ipswich and when the railway arrived.

Much of the town's history and legacy are brought vividly to life in the splendid *Museum of East Anglian Life*, which is situated in the centre of town to the west of the market place, in a 70-acre meadowland site on the old Abbot's Hall Estate (the aisled original barn dates from the 13th century). Part of the open-air section features several historic buildings which have been moved from elsewhere in the region and carefully re-erected on site. These include an engineering workshop from the 1870s, part of a 14th century farmhouse, a watermill from Alton and a wind pump which was rescued in a collapsed state at Minsmere in 1977.

There's also a collection of working steam engines, farm animals and year-round demonstrations of all manner of local arts and crafts, from coopering to candle-making, from sheep shearing to saddlery.

Stowmarket's Church of St Peter and St Mary acquired a new spire in 1994, replacing the 1715 version (itself a replacement) which was dismantled on safety grounds in 1975.

The town certainly merits a major stroll, while for a peaceful picnic the riverbank beckons. Serious scenic walkers should make for the *Gipping Valley River Park* walk, which runs all the way to Ipswich.

Around Stowmarket

Buxhall   *Map 2 ref E6*
3 miles W of Stowmarket just off the B1115

The village church is notable for its six heavy bells, but the best-known landmark in this quiet village is undoubtedly the majestic tower mill, without sails since a gale removed them in 1929 but still standing as a silent, sturdy reminder of its working days. This is good walking country, with an ancient wood and many signposted footpaths.

Needham Market   *Map 2 ref F6*
4 miles SE of Stowmarket off the A14

A thriving village whose greatest glory is the wonderful carvings on the ceiling of the **Church of St John the Baptist**. The church, both outside and within, is otherwise not remarkable, so the ornate double hammerbeam roof seems all the more magnificent, especially when bathed in light from the strategically placed skylight. The roof is massive, as high as the walls of the church itself; the renowned authority on Suffolk churches, H Munro Cautley, described the work at Needham as *"the culminating achievement of the English carpenter"*.

The River Gipping flows to the east of the High Street and its banks provide miles of walks: the towpath is a public right of way walkable all the way from Stowmarket to Ipswich and the on riverbank at Needham is a 25-acre picnic site and a nature reserve.

Nearby Barking, on the B1018 south of Needham, was once more important than its neighbour, being described in 1874 as *"a pleasant village ... including the hamlet of Needham Market"*. This explains the fact that Barking's church is exceptionally large for a village church: it was the mother church to Needham Market and was used for Needham's burials when that place has no ground of its own.

Baylham   *Map 2 ref F7*
7 miles SE of Stowmarket off the B1113

The Roman site of *Combretrovium* is home to **Baylham House Rare Breeds Farm**, and visitors (April-early October) will find displays and information relating to both Rome and rare animals. The farm's chief concern is the survival of rare breeds and there are breeding groups of cattle, sheep, pigs, goats and poultry.

Great and Little Blakenham
Map 2 ref F7
8 miles SE of Stowmarket on the B1113

A short way south lie the twin villages of Great and Little Blakenham, Little with a five-acre bluebell wood open Wednesday, Thursday and Sunday in the summer.

Barham
Map 2 ref G7
8 miles SE of Stowmarket off the A14

On the other side of the A14 are the villages of Claydon and Barham, the latter's church serving both villages. One of the windows in the vestry dates from the 16th century and a fine brass is dated 1514.

The Sorrel Horse lies by the Old Norwich Road in an agreeable country setting. Behind the pub are lawns and gardens with a profusion of colourful flowers and plants. Chairs, tables and umbrellas by the dozen are a boon on sunny days, and children are kept busy with a variety of slides and playthings. An L-shaped wooden counter serves the bar, where open fireplaces, original beams (walls and ceiling) and low rustic chairs and tables paint a traditional scene. There's a large framed collection of banknotes and cigarette cards. Bar snacks and à la carte lunches are available, and there are two cosy seating areas.

Away from the main building owners Bridget (Breda) Smith and her sons Matthew and Philip have recently expanded the scope of their pub by converting an old barn to provide bed and breakfast

The Sorrel Horse

accommodation in eight bedrooms. Conservation laws decree that the barn's exterior should stay in its original state, but inside all is stylishly state-of-the-art. Six of the rooms, including one adapted for disabled guests, have their own private facilities, while the other two (a single and a family room) share a bathroom and may be booked as one. *The Sorrel Horse, Old Norwich Road, Barham, Suffolk, IP6 0PG. Tel: 01473 830327*

Bramford

Map 2 ref G7

11 miles SE of Stowmarket off the A14

Bramford, a mile or so further on along the A14, has a pretty little church, St Mary's, with a 13th century stone screen. It was once an important spot on the river route, when barges from Ipswich stopped to unload corn; the walls of the old lock are still visible. In the vicinity is *Suffolk Water Park*, where the lake welcomes canoeists and windsurfers.

Earl Stonham

Map 2 ref G6

6 miles E of Stowmarket on the A1120

A scattered village set around three greens in farming land. The Church of St Mary the Virgin boasts one of Suffolk's finest single hammerbeam roofs, and is also notable for its Bible scene murals, the doom (Last Judgement scene) over the chancel arch and a triple hour-glass, presumably to record just how protracted were some of the sermons.

Stonham Aspal

Map 2 ref G6

7 miles E of Stowmarket on the A1120

On the other side of the A140 lies Stonham Aspal, where in 1962 the remains of a Roman bath house were unearthed. The parish church has an unusual wooden top to its tower, a necessary addition to house the ten bells that a keen campanologist insisted on installing. At Stonham Barns, the *British Birds of Prey and Nature Centre* (Tel: 01449 711425) is home to every British owl and raptors from Britain and around the world. These wonderful birds flap their wings in regular flying displays, and in the Pets Paradise the kiddies can say hello to the hamsters and horses, the mice and the meerkats, the parrots and the piglets.

Maria and Charles Tydeman's *Barn Cottages* offer self-catering accommodation in the most delightful surroundings. The five cottages, with black weatherboarded walls and tiled roofs, all face south, with access to a picturesque cottage garden set in four acres of tranquil grounds. All the cottages have twin or double bedrooms

Barn Cottages

and well-equipped kitchen/diners, plus a full range of accessories to guarantee a comfortable, do-as-you-please stay. Facilities in the village include a garden centre, pub and tennis court, and the road network provides easy access to the sights of Suffolk. The cottages are available throughout the year. Pets by prior arrangement. *Barn Cottages,'Goldings', East End Lane, Stonham Aspal, Near Stowmarket, Suffolk, 1P14 6AS. Tel: 01449 711229 E-Mail: Maria@Barncottages.Demon.Co.UK*

Ashfield   *Map 2 ref H5*
10 miles E of Stowmarket off the A1120
A mile or two further along the A1120 lies Pettaugh and, beyond it, Ashfield. Motorists and cyclists on the A1120 Stowmarket-Yoxford road provide plenty of passing trade for Peter and Lynda van Dijk's **Swan Craft Gallery**. It's a great place to break your journey, and

Swan Craft Gallery

the reward is a veritable Aladdin's cave of local crafts, with ceramics, jewellery, pressed flowers and greetings cards among the goods ranged in profusion on the shelves. The buildings have plenty of character, dating from about 1640 and seeing service as an inn and a private dwelling before adopting their current role. The shop itself is built in a former stable and features low beamed ceilings. The owners have plans to add to the appeal of the Gallery by opening a tea shop. *Swan Craft Gallery, Roman Road, Ashfield, Nr Stowmarket, Suffolk, IP14 6LU. Tel: 01728 685703*

Another very good reason for pausing awhile in Ashfield is to call in at **Deben Valley Nurseries**, one mile from Debenham, close to the River Deben and just off the main road. Doreen Read, a member of the Horticultural Trades Association, runs the business on her own in a very friendly and relaxed way, catering admirably for

the growing band of DIY gardening enthusiasts and opening from 10 till 5 Tuesday to Sunday (plus Bank Holiday Mondays) between March and December. There's ample parking space and easy access for loading the car, and children threatening to sow the seeds of impatience while their parents select their plants and garden accessories can be steered towards the birds in their aviaries and the Shetland ponies. The range of items for sale is impressive, from herbs

Deben Valley Nurseries

and heathers, house plants and hanging baskets through fuchsias and floral gifts to trees and climbers, garden ornaments, compost and gro-bags. Visitors looking for a present and unable to make a decision can take the easy way out with a National Garden gift token. *Deben Valley Nurseries, Thorpe Lane, Ashfield, Suffolk, IP14 6NE. Tel/Fax: 01728 860559*

Earl Soham
Map 3 ref H5

12 miles E of Stowmarket on the A1120

Earl Soham, a couple of miles east of Ashfield, comprises a long, winding street that was once part of a Roman road. It lies in a valley, and on the largest of its three greens the village sign is a carved wooden statue of a falconer given as a gift by the Womens Institute in 1953. The 13th century Church of St Mary is well worth a visit.

Saxtead Green   *Map 3 ref H5*
14 miles E of Stowmarket off the A1120

One of the prettiest sights in Suffolk is the white *18th century mill* that stands on the marshy green. This is a wonderful example of a post mill, perhaps the best in the world, dating back to 1796 and renovated first in the 19th century. She worked until 1947 and has since been kept in working order, with the sails turning though the mill no longer grinds. You can climb into the buck (body) of the elegant weatherboarded construction and explore the machinery. It's open for visits in the summer (Tel: 01728 685789).

On the green at Saxtead, just 200 yards from the famous mill and not far from Framlingham Castle, *Ivy Forge*, owned and run by George and Margaret Martin, offers bed and breakfast accommodation with an evening meal by arrangement (2 or 3 days' notice when booking, then on the day). Dinner makes good use of home-

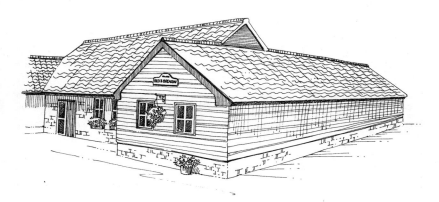

Ivy Forge

grown vegetables and the baking is done on the premises. No trace of the old farm forge survives, but the current modern single-storey building, in a conservation area, looks the part with black weatherboarding on two of its three sides. It surrounds a sun-trap courtyard, and there's also an attractive garden. Breakfast is as light or as hearty as you like. No smoking. *Ivy Forge, The Green, Saxtead, Near Framlingham, Suffolk, IP13 9QG. Tel: 01728 685054*

Framlingham

The marvellous *castle*, brooding on a hilltop, dominates this agreeable market town, as it has since Roger Bigod, 2nd Earl of Norfolk, built it in the 12th century (his grandfather built the first a century earlier but this wooden construction was soon demolished). The Earls and Dukes of Norfolk, the Howards, were here for many generations before moving to Arundel in 1635. The castle is in remarkably good condition, partly because it was rarely attacked – though King John put it under siege in 1215. Its most famous occupant was Mary Tudor, who was in residence when proclaimed Queen in 1553. In the reign of Elizabeth I it was used as a prison for defiant priests and in the 17th century, after being bequeathed to Pembroke College, Cambridge, it saw service as a home and school for local paupers. Nine of the castle's 13 towers are accessible and the climb up the spiral staircase and walk round the battlements are well worth the effort. On one side the view is of the meres, which is a bird sanctuary. In the north wing is the Lanman Museum, devoted to farm and craft tools and domestic bygones.

The castle brought considerable prestige and prosperity to Framlingham, evidence of which can be found in the splendid *Church of St Michael*, which has two wonderful works of art. One is the tomb of Henry Fitzroy, bastard son of Henry VIII, beautifully adorned with scenes from Genesis and Exodus and in a superb state of repair. The other is the tomb of the 3rd Duke with carvings of the apostles in shell niches. Also of note is the Carolean organ of 1674, a gift of Sir Robert Hitcham, to whom the Howards sold the estate. Cromwell and the Puritans were anti-organ so this instrument was lucky to escape the mass destruction of organs at the time of the Commonwealth. Sir Robert is also buried in the church. On a humbler level, the people of Framlingham are very proud of their two Victorian post boxes, which were installed in 1856.

Around Framlingham

A mile north of Framlingham on the B1120 is *Shawsgate Vineyard* (Tel: 01728 724060), a 15-acre site established in 1973. Besides tours and tastings there are various vines for sale, and for a really different idea you can lease a row of vines and have the grapes from that row made into your very own wine. There's a children's play area and a picnic area.

Dennington
Map 3 ref I5

2 miles N of Framlingham on the B1116

Continuing the postal theme, the pretty little village of Dennington boasts one of the oldest post offices in the country, this one having occupied the same site since 1830. The village *church* has some very unusual features, none more so than the hanging pyx canopy above the altar. A pyx served as a receptacle for the Reserved Sacrament which would be kept under a canopy attached to weights and pulleys so that the whole thing could be lowered when the sacrament was required for the sick and the dying.

The church also has many interesting carvings, the most remarkable being that of a skiapod, the only known representation in this county of a mythical creature of the African desert, humanoid but with a huge boat-shaped foot with which he could cover himself against the sun. This curious beast was 'known' to Herodotus and to Pliny, who remarked that it had *'great pertinacity in leaping'*. In the chapel at the top of the south aisle stands the tomb of Lord Bardolph, who fought at Agincourt, and his wife, their effigies carved in alabaster.

Charsfield
Map 3 ref H6

5 miles S of Framlington off the B1078

A minor road runs from Framlingham through picturesque Kettleburgh and Hoo to Charsfield, best known as the inspiration for Ronald Blyth's book *Akenfield*, later memorably filmed by Sir Peter Hall. A cottage garden in the village displays the Akenfield village sign and is open to visitors in the summer.

Otley
Map 2 ref H6

7 miles SW of Framlingham on the B1079

The 15th century *moated hall* is open to the public at certain times (Tel: 01473 890264). Standing in ten acres of gardens that include a canal, a nuttery and a knot garden, the hall was long associated with the Gosnold family, whose coat of arms is also that of the village. The best-known member of that family is Bartholomew Gosnold, who sailed to the New World, named Martha's Vineyard, discovered Cape Cod and founded the settlement of Jamestown, Virginia. The 13th century Church of St Mary has a remarkable baptistry font measuring 6 feet in length and 2 feet 8 inches in depth. Though filled with water, the font is not used and was only discovered in 1950 when the vestry floor was raised. Perhaps it was used for adult baptisms.

Helmingham
Map 2 ref H6

7 miles W of Framlingham on the B1077

Another moated hall, this one a Tudor construction. The house is not open to the public but on summer Sundays the gardens can be visited; attractions include herbaceous and spring borders, many varieties of rose, safari rides and deer, Highland cattle and Soay sheep. The Tollemache family were here for many years, and one of their number founded a brewery, which, after a merger, became the Tolly Cobbold brewery based in Ipswich.

Framsden
Map 2 ref H6

7 miles W of Framlingham on the B1077

The scenery in these parts is real picture postcard stuff, and in the village of Framsden the picture is completed by a fine *post mill*, this one built high on a hill in 1760, refitted and raised in 1836 and in commercial use until 1934. The milling machinery is still in place and the mill is open for visits at weekends by appointment only (Tel: 01473 890328).

Cretingham
Map 3 ref H6

4 miles W of Framlingham off the A1120

The village sign is the unusual item here, in that it has two different panels: one shows an everyday Anglo-Saxon farming scene, the other a group (of Danes?) sailing up the River Deben, with the locals fleeing. The signs are made from mosaic tiles.

Brandeston
Map 3 ref H6

3 miles W of Framlingham off the A1120

A further mile to the east, through more pretty countryside, Brandeston is another delightful spot, with a row of beautiful thatched cottages and the parish Church of All Saints with a 13th century font.

The best-known vicar of Brandeston was John Lowes (1572-1646) who was accused of witchcraft by the villagers, interrogated by Witchfinder General Matthew Hopkins and hanged at Bury St Edmunds. His sad end was made even sadder by the fact that before being strung up he had himself to read out the burial service of a condemned witch, as no priest was allowed to conduct the service. Hopkins made a handsome living out of this bizarre business, preying on the superstitions of the times and using the foulest means to obtain confessions. One account of his end is that he himself was accused of being a witch and hanged. The less satisfactory alternative is that he died of tuberculosis. Witch do you prefer?

Debenham

Map 2 ref G5

10 miles E of Stowmarket on the B1077

A sizeable village of architectural distinction, with a profusion of attractive timber-framed buildings dating from the 14th to the 17th century. The River Deben flows beside and beneath the main street and, by one of the little bridges, weavers still practise their craft.

High Street, Debenham

There is also a pottery centre. St Mary's Church is unusual in having an original Saxon tower, and the roof alternates hammerbeams and crested tie beams.

Mendlesham

Map 2 ref F5

6 miles NE of Stowmarket off the A140

On the green in Old Market Street lies an enormous stone which is said to have been used as a preaching stone, mounted by itinerant Wesleyan preachers. In the Church of St Mary there is a collection of parish armour assembled 400 years ago, and also some fine carvings. The least hidden local landmark is a 1,000ft TV mast put up by the IBA in 1959.

Wetheringsett

Map 2 ref G5

7 miles NE of Stowmarket off the A140

On the other side of the A140, Wetheringsett is where you'll find **Mid-Suffolk Light Railway Museum**, open on summer Sundays and during summer school holidays.

Wetheringsett has had two well-known rectors, famous for very different reasons. Richard Hakluyt, incumbent from 1590 to 1616, is remembered for his major work *Voyages* (full title *Principal Navigation, Voiages, Traffiques and Discoveries of the English Nation*).

The rector between 1858 and 1883 was a certain George Wilfrid Ellis, sometime tailor and butler, and finally a bogus clergyman. After he was unmasked as a sham it needed a special Act of Parliament to validate the marriage ceremonies he had illegally conducted and to legitimise the issue of those marriages.

Thornham Magna & Parva   Map 2 ref F4
10 miles N of Stowmarket off the A140
The **Thornham Walks and Field Centre**, with 12 miles of walks and a herb garden and nursery, cater admirably for hikers, horticulturists and students of the countryside. The tiny thatched Church of St Mary at Thornham Parva houses a considerable treasure in the shape of an exquisite medieval altar painting, known as a retable, with a central panel depicting the Crucifixion and four saints on each side panel. Its origins are uncertain but it was possibly the work of the Royal Workshops at Westminster Abbey, and made for Thetford Priory, or a nearby Dominican monastery. Also to be admired is the 14th century octagonal font and a series of fascinating wall paintings. In the churchyard is a monument to Sir Basil Spence (1907-76), architect of Coventry Cathedral.

Yaxley   Map 2 ref G4
12 miles NE of Stowmarket on the A140
Another **Church of St Mary** and more treasures. One is an extremely rare sexton's wheel, which hangs above the south door and was used in medieval times to select fast days in honour of the Virgin. When a pair of iron wheels were spun on their axle, strings attached to the outer wheel would catch on the inner, stopping both and indicating the chosen day. The 17th century pulpit is one of the finest in the country, with the most glorious, sumptuous carvings.

Yaxley's most famous son is Sir Frederick Ashton, who is buried in the churchyard.

Eye   Map 2 ref G4
13 miles NE of Stowmarket on the B1117
The name is derived from the Saxon for an island, as this super little town was once surrounded by water and marshes. The **Church of St Peter and St Paul** stands in the shadow of a mound on which a castle once stood (the remains are worth a look and the mound offers a panoramic view of the town – almost a bird's eye view, in fact). The church's 100 foot tower is described by Pevsner as *"one of the wonders of Suffolk"* and the interior is a masterpiece of restoration, with all the essential medieval features in place. The rood

screen, with painted panels depicting St Edmund, St Ursula, Edward the Confessor and Henry VI, is particularly fine.

Other interesting Eye sights are the ornate redbrick town hall; the timbered Guildhall, with the archangel Gabriel carved on a corner post; a crinkle-crankle (serpentine) wall fronting Chandos Lodge, where Sir Frederick Ashton once lived; and a thriving theatre, one of the smallest professional theatres in the country.

Around Eye

Hoxne *Map 2 ref G3*
4 miles NE of Eye on the B1118
Palaeolithic remains indicate the exceptionally long history of Hoxne (call it Hoxon), which stands along the banks of the River Waveney near the Norfolk border. It is best known for its links with King Edmund, who was reputedly killed here, though Bradfield St Clare has a rival claim. The Hoxne legend is that Edmund was betrayed to the Danes by a newlywed couple who were crossing the Goldbrook bridge and spotted his golden spurs reflected from his hiding place below the bridge. Edmund put a curse on all newlyweds crossing the bridge, and to this day some brides take care to avoid it.

The story continues that Edmund was tied to an oak tree and killed with arrows. That same oak mysteriously fell down in 1848 while apparently in good health, and a monument at the site is a popular tourist attraction. In the Church of St Peter and St Paul an oak screen (perhaps that very same oak?) depicts scenes from the martyr's life. A more cheerful event is the Harvest Breakfast on the village green that follows the annual service.

Horham *Map 2 ref H4*
6 miles E of Eye on the B1117
Three distinct musical connections in this dapper little village. The Norman church has had its tower strengthened for the rehanging of the peal of eight bells, which is believed to be the oldest in the world. Benjamin Britten, later associated with the Aldeburgh Festival, lived and composed in Horham for a time, and on a famous day during World War II, Glenn Miller brought his band here to celebrate the 200th flying mission from the American aerodrome.

Worlingworth *Map 3 ref H5*
8 miles SE of Eye off the B1118
It's well worth taking the country road to Worlingworth, a long, straggling village whose Church of St Mary has a remarkable font cover

reaching up about 30 feet. It is brilliantly coloured and intricately carved, and near the top is an inscription in Greek which translates as *'wash my sin and not my body only'*. Note, too, the Carolean box pews, the carved pulpit and an oil painting of Worlingworth's Great Feast of 1810 to celebrate George III's jubilee.

Wingfield
Map 3 ref H3
6 miles E of Eye off the B1118
Wingfield College is one of the country's most historic seats of learning, founded in 1362 as a college for priests with a bequest from Sir John de Wingfield, Chief Staff Officer to the Black Prince. Sir John's wealth came from ransoming a French nobleman at the Battle of Poitiers in 1356. Surrendered to Henry VIII at the time of the Dissolution, the college became a farmhouse and is now in private hands. The facade is now Georgian, but the original medieval Great Hall still stands, and the college and its three acres of gardens are open to the public at weekends during the summer. Attractions include regular artistic events and printing demonstrations.

The Church of St Andrew was built as the collegiate church and has an extra-large chancel to accommodate the college choir. The church contains three really fine monuments: to Sir John (in stone); to Michael de la Pole, 2nd Earl of Suffolk (in wood); and to John de la Pole, Duke of Suffolk (in alabaster). In the churchyard is a hudd – a shelter for the priest for use at the graveside in bad weather.

On a hill outside the village are the imposing remains of a castle built by the 1st Earl.

Fressingfield
Map 3 ref H3
10 miles E of Eye on the B1116
The Fox and Goose restaurant is one of the best in Suffolk, but the spiritual centre is the Church of St Peter and St Paul. It has a superb hammerbeam roof and a lovely stone bell tower that was built in the 14th century. On one of the pews the initials AP are carved. These are believed to be the work of Alice de la Pole, Duchess of Norfolk and grand-daughter of Geoffrey Chaucer. Was this a work of art or a bout of vandalism brought on by a dull sermon?

At nearby **Ufford Hall** lived the Sancroft family, one of whom became Archbishop of Canterbury. He led the revolt of the bishops against James II and was imprisoned in the Tower of London. Released by William IV and sacked for refusing to swear the oath of allegiance, he returned home and is entombed by the south porch of the church.

The village sign is a pilgrim and a donkey, recording that Fressingfield was a stopping place on the pilgrim route from Dunwich to Bury St Edmunds.

Laxfield

Map 3 ref I4

12 miles E of Eye on the B1117

Laxfield & District Museum, in the 16th century Guildhall, gives a fine insight into bygone ages with geology and natural history exhibits, farm and domestic tools, a Victorian kitchen, a village shop and a costume room. The museum is open Saturday and Sunday afternoons in summer.

All Saints Church is distinguished by some wonderful flint flashwork on its tower, roof and nave. In the 1808 Baptist church is

Laxfield Guildhall

a plaque remembering John Noyes, burnt at the stake in 1557 for refusing to take Catholic vows. History relates that the villagers, with a single exception, dowsed their fires in protest, and the one remaining fire was used to light the stake.

A couple of miles east of Laxfield, Heveningham Hall is a fine Georgian mansion, a model of classical elegance designed by James Wyatt with lovely grounds by Capability Brown. As it runs through the grounds, the River Blyth widens into a lake.

CHAPTER FOUR
Northeast Suffolk

Herringfleet Mill

Chapter 4 - Area Covered

For precise location of places please refer to the colour maps found at the rear of the book.

4
Northeast Suffolk

Introduction

While inland Suffolk has few peers in terms of picturesque country-side and villages, Suffolk is also very much a maritime county, with over 50 miles of coastline. All those miles have been constantly bombarded by the North Sea, and out at sea the sandbanks have often proved disastrous to shipping; at one time as many wrecks were recorded here as anywhere around Britain's shores.

The Romans built a series of signal stations, and the Suffolk coast was the first to be systematically lighted, starting with twin lights at Lowestoft in 1609. The whole coastline has been subject to erosion (and is in any case sinking as Scotland rises) and several communities have disappeared completely under the waves. The estuaries of the Waveney, Blyth, Alde, Deben, Orwell and Stour have somewhat minimised the erosion, and the whole stretch is a marvellous mixture of estuaries, beaches, marshes, reedland, heath and pasture. In 1993 the Suffolk Coast and Heath Project was created to protect and conserve this area of outstanding natural beauty, which is home to an amazing variety of flora and fauna. The whole coast is a conservation area, which the 50-mile Suffolk Coastal Path makes walkable throughout.

With all the miles of meandering rivers and superb stretches of coastline, it is only natural that watery pursuits are a popular pastime, and everything from sailing to scuba diving, from angling to powerboat racing, is available. Many of the local museums have a nautical theme, and the Suffolk coast has been a source of inspiration for many of our most distinguished writers and composers.

Halesworth

Granted a market in 1222, Halesworth reached the peak of its trading importance when the River Blyth was made navigable as far as the town in 1756. A stroll around the streets reveals several buildings of architectural interest. The Market Place has a handsome Elizabethan timber-framed house, but the chief attraction for the visitor is the *Halesworth and District Museum* at Steeple End, a conversion of a row of 17th century almshouses. Local geology and archaeology are the main interests, with various fossils and flints on display, and there's a fascinating account of the Halesworth witchcraft trials of 1645. An art gallery is in the same building.

Among Halesworth's distinguished inhabitants were Sir William Jackson Hooker and his son Sir Joseph Dalton Hooker, renowned botanists who were the first two directors of the Royal Botanical Gardens at Kew. They lived at Brewery House, which still stands, though its gardens have not survived.

Bramfield   *Map 4 ref J4*
3 miles S of Halesworth on the A144

The massive Norman round tower of *St Andrew's Church* is separate from the main building and was built as a defensive structure, with walls over 3 feet thick. Dowsing ran riot here in 1643, destroyed 24 superstitious pictures, one crucifix and picture of Christ, and 12 angels on the roof. The most important monument is one to Sir Arthur Coke, sometime Lord Chief Justice, who died in 1629, and his wife Elizabeth. Arthur is kneeling, resplendent in full armour, while Elizabeth is lying on her bed with a baby in her arms. This monument is the work of Nicholas Stone, the most important English mason and sculptor of his day. The Cokes at one time occupied Bramfield Hall, and another family, in residence for 300 years, were the Rabetts, whose coat of arms in the church punningly depicts rabbits on its shield.

Mark Corcoran at the stoves and Amanda front of house make a winning combination at *The Queen's Head*, a venerable and much-loved hostelry set in a large ornamental garden next to the thatched church with its unusual separate bell tower. There's plenty of outside bench seating, with an area for children in the garden (safely away from the cars), while the activity inside focuses on an amazing barn with a vast, lofty ceiling, interesting beams, old pews at rustic tables and what must be a contender for the largest open hearth in the land. Home-made food is taken very seriously here, the high-

The Queen's Head

light being roast rare breeds of beef, lamb and pork, expertly prepared by a local butcher and cooked to perfection to form the centrepiece of Sunday lunch. Home-made ice cream is another speciality and the selection, which changes all the time, could include toffee and hazelnut, marmalade, lemon meringue or rhubarb crumble. *The Queen's Head, The Street, Bramfield, Near Halesworth, Suffolk, IP19 9HT. Tel: 01986 784214*

Holton St Peter
Map 4 ref J3
1 mile E of Halesworth on the B1123
A splendid little post mill built in 1750 nestles in a pine forest above the village. To arrange a visit call 01986 872367. Look in also at the Church of St Peter, which has a round Norman tower, a 15th century octagonal font and a 16th century pulpit.

Ilketshall St Lawrence
Map 4 ref J2
5 miles N of Halesworth on the A144
The church here is in simple, ancient style. It dates from the 12th century and stands on a mound reputed to be an old Roman staging post – certainly it lies on the Roman road that connected Halesworth and Bungay. Some Roman bricks have been found in the east end of the chancel.

Bungay
Map 4 ref I2
9 miles N of Halesworth on the A144
An ancient fortress town on the River Waveney. The river played an important part in the town's fortunes until well into the 18th cen-

tury, with barges laden with coal, corn, malt and timber plying the route to the coast. The river is no longer navigable above Geldeston but is a great attraction for anglers and yachtsmen.

Bungay is best known for its *castle*, built in its original form by Hugh Bigod, 1st Earl of Norfolk, as a rival to Henry II's castle at Orford. In 1173 Hugh took the side of the rebellious sons of Henry, but this insurrection ended with the surrender of the castle to the king. Hugh was killed not long after this episode while on the Third Crusade; his son Roger inherited the

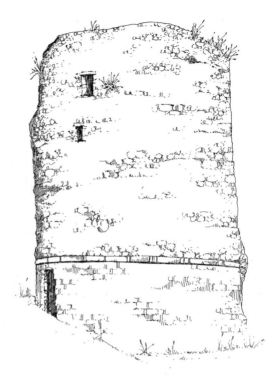

Bigod Castle, Bungay

title and the castle, but it was another Roger Bigod who came to Bungay in 1294 and built the round tower and mighty outer walls which stand today.

To the north of the castle are Bungay's two surviving churches of note (the Domesday Book recorded five). The Saxon round tower of *Holy Trinity Church* is the oldest complete structure in the town, and a brass plate on the door commemorates the church's narrow escape from the fire of 1688 that destroyed much of the town (similar disasters overtook many other towns with close-set timber-and-thatch buildings). The *Church of St Mary* – now redundant – was not so lucky, being more or less completely gutted. The tower survives to dominate the townscape, and points of interest in the church itself include a woodcarving of the Resurrection presented by Rider Haggard, and a monument to General Robert Kelso, who fought in the American War of Independence.

A century before the fire the church received a visit, during a storm, from the devilish Black Shuck, a retriever-like hound who, hot from causing severe damage at Blythburgh, raced down the nave and killed two worshippers. A weather vane in the market place puts the legend into verse:

> *"All down the church in midst of fire*
> *The Hellish Monster Flew*
> *And Passing onwards to the Quire*
> *He many people slew."*

Nearby is the famous octagonal **Butter Cross**, rebuilt after the Great Fire and topped by Justice with her scales and sword. This building was once used as a prison, with a dungeon below.

Tramping the Bungay Town Trail can be thirsty work, so what could be better for recharging the batteries than to pause in a pub where they brew their own beer! **The Green Dragon**, a convivial two-bar hostelry on the northern edge of town, is just such a place, and since 1991 brothers Rob (the brewer) and William (the chef) Pickard have provided splendid liquid and solid sustenance to lucky locals and tourists. The brewery is in a converted barn at the back and it's well worth while making an appointment to have a look round. The product is excellent and Rob has won prizes at beer festivals. His brews include Mild, Chaucer Ale, Bridge Street Bitter and Dragon - the last is pretty potent, so the high-backed chairs at

The Green Dragon

the bar counter can definitely come in useful! Food enjoys equal billing at this delightful place, with home-made pizzas, fish and chips, and authentic curries among the favourites, and speciality evenings on Wednesdays and Fridays. An impressive wine list offers plenty of alternatives to the real ales.

The main bar has leaded windows and a rich red colour scheme, while green is the predominant colour in the public bar. A green dragon in stained glass adorns the most unusual mirror and there are representations of green dragons everywhere, along with pictures of old buses and old regulars, plus shelves full of jugs and pots and ancient bottles. Open fires add to the cheerful scene, while outside, the large garden has wooden tables and chairs, making it a fine spot for families and summer sipping. The brothers keep their customers well informed by means of a notice board which details such activities as cricket club functions and overseas beer trips. *The Green Dragon, 29 Broad Street, Bungay, Suffolk, NR35 1EE. Tel: 01986 892681*

Around Bungay

Earsham
Map 4 ref I2

1 mile SW of Bungay off the A143

All Saints Church and Earsham Hall are well worth a visit, but what brings most people here is the **Otter Trust**, on the banks of the Waveney, where the largest collection of otters in natural enclosures are bred for re-introduction into the wild. Waterfowl, herons are deer are also kept here, and there are some lovely walks by the lakes and river. Tel: 01986 893470.

Flixton
Map 4 ref I2

2 miles SW of Bungay on the B1062

Javelin, Meteor, Sea Vixen, Westland Whirlwind: names that evoke earlier days of flying, and just four of the 20 aircraft on show at The **Norfolk and Suffolk Aviation Museum**, on the site of a USAAF Liberator base in World War II. There's a lot of associated material, both civil and military, covering the period from World War I to the present day. The museum incorporates the Royal Observer Corps Museum, RAF Bomber Command Museum, and the Museum and Memorial of the 446th Bomb Group – the *Bungay Buckeroos*.

Flixton is named after St Flik, the first Bishop of East Anglia, and he is depicted in the village sign.

Mendham
Map 4 ref H3
6 miles SW of Bungay off the A143

This pretty little village on the Waveney is the birthplace of Sir Alfred Munnings RA, who was born at Mendham Mill, where his father was the miller. Sir Alfred's *Charlotte and her Pony* was the inspiration for the village sign, which was unveiled by his niece Kathleen Hadingham.

Beccles
Map 4 ref J2
11 miles N of Halesworth on the A145

The largest town in the Waveney district at the southernmost point of the Broads. The Saxons were here, the Vikings were here, and at one time the market was a major supplier of herring (up to 60,000 a year) to the Abbey at Bury St Edmunds. At the height of its trading importance Beccles must have painted a splendidly animated picture, with wherries constantly on the move transporting goods from seaports to inland town. The same stretch of river is still alive, but now with the yachts and pleasure boats of the holidaymakers and weekenders who fill the town in summer. The regatta in July and August is a particularly busy time.

The fires that are such a sadly common part of small-town history ravaged Beccles at various times in the 16th and 17th centuries, destroying much of the old town. For that reason the dwellings are largely Georgian in origin, with handsome redbrick facades. One that is not is **Roos Hall**, a gabled building dating from 1583. Just outside the town, far enough away to escape the great fire of 1586, it was built to a Dutch design, underlining the links between East Anglia and the Low Countries forged by the wool and weaving trades. Elizabeth I stayed at the hall just after it was completed, when she visited Beccles to present the town's charter; the occasion is depicted in the town sign. One of the hall's owners was Sir John Suckling (later to become Controller of the Household to James I), one of whose descendants was Lord Nelson. Any old hall worth its salt has a ghost, and the Roos representative is a headless coachman who appears on Christmas Eve.

The parish **Church of St Michael** was built in the second half of the 14th century by the Abbot of Bury. Its tower stands separate, built in the 16th century, rising almost 100 feet and containing a peal of bells. An unusual feature at the north facade is an outside pulpit taking the form of a small balcony. The priest could enter the pulpit from inside the church and preach to lepers, who were not allowed inside. Nelson's parents, the Reverend Edmund Nelson and

Catherine Suckling, were married in St Michael's, so too the Suffolk poet George Crabbe, of whom much more in Chapter 5.

Another building with Dutch-style gables houses **Beccles & District Museum**, whose contents include 19th century toys and costume, farm implements, items from the old town jail and memorabilia from the sailing wherries. There's also a model of the town in 1841 and some early printing presses. Tel: 01502 715722.

Beccles, like Bungay, is a printing town, and has its own **printing museum** at the Newgate works of printer William Clowes. Here the visitor will learn about the history of printing since the 1800s, with woodcuts, books and machinery, and it is also possible to tour the factory. Tel: 01502 712884.

A mile south of Beccles in the small hamlet of Weston on the A145 Blythburgh road stands **Winter Flora**, a flower shop and garden of outstanding beauty and interest. A large, custom-built shop houses a wonderful selection of dried and silk flowers, artistically displayed on attractive glass or wooden stands against hand-painted

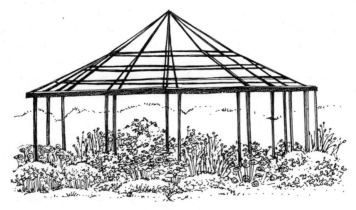

Winter Flora

backcloths. Apart from flowers there are wicker baskets, glass and ceramic pots, ornamental candles, exotics from around the world, and even zany Chinese scarecrows.

The garden was designed to enhance the appearance of the shop and to show the plants which are for sale in a garden setting. Each bed has its own colour theme, with blue running happily through much of the garden. The herb garden is one of many splendid features and an absolute must for visitors to see. A little pine-furnished coffee shop offers a small range of delicious home-made cakes, soup, rolls and cheese. Jane Seppings run this truly delightful place with friendly staff and a lovable cat called Poppett. Winter Flora is open from 10 till 5 daily (Sunday till 4). *Winter Flora Ltd, Hall Farm, Weston, Near Beccles, Suffolk, NR34 8TT. Tel: 01502 716810 (shop) 713346 (office)*

Around Beccles

Toft Monks   *Map 4 ref J1*
4 miles N of Beccles on the A143

Enterprising owners Jan and Giles Mortimer, who arrived here in March 1997, have created a perfect stopover in Toft Monks, a village on the A143 north of Beccles and just over the border in Norfolk.

The white-painted *Toft Lion* is nothing if not versatile, with real ales, cold snacks and home-cooked meals, pool table and darts, pétanque in the garden, easy parking a letting bedroom for overnight stays. A beer festival takes place in August, and a carol concert is held a few days before Christmas. The printed menu of sandwiches, salads and hot main courses (always something for vegetarians) is supplemented by blackboard specials, and meals are taken in a delightful little country kitchen-style dining area whose ceiling is hung with mugs. The bars are filled with interesting bric-a-brac, from brasses and farm implements to sepia pictures of the

The Toft Lion

original building and a collection of matchboxes to light up any philumenist's day. Two sofas by the brick-breasted open fire are particularly tempting spots for whiling away an hour or two in convivial company. Well-behaved children and dogs are welcome. *The Toft Lion, Toft Monks, Near Beccles, Norfolk, NR34 0EP. Tel: 01502 677702*

Burgh St Peter   Map 4 ref K1
6 miles NE of Beccles off the A143

The **Waveney River Centre** is a riverside complex 1½ miles from the village of Burgh St Peter Staithe, 4 miles through country lanes from the A143 Beccles-Great Yarmouth road. It's a place of many and varied attractions: large grounds with space and amenities for 60 caravans and room for campers; a fully equipped marina that can accommodate up to 60 yachts; a leisure centre with gym, sauna and heated indoor swimming pool; and a mini-market selling foodstuffs, boat equipment, fishing gear, and fuel. The heart of the complex is a 150-year-old free house with a bar menu, a carvery, and an extensive à la carte menu. Owners Tony and Wanphen Mar-

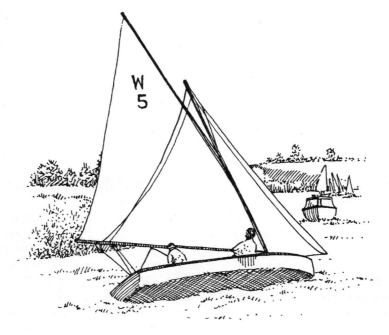

River Waveney

The Waveney River Centre

tin have lived in Spain, Thailand, Mexico, Malaysia and Turkey, and at weekends they host international theme nights featuring cuisine from all those places and many more besides. There's a family room with a variety of games as well as an outside play area and tables overlooking the river and marshes. *Waveney River Centre, Burgh St Peter Staithe, Burgh St Peter, Near Beccles, Norfolk, NR34 0BT. Tel: 01502 677217*

Ringsfield   Map 4 ref J2
2 miles SW of Beccles off the A146

In a wooded valley away from the main village, the parish Church of All Saints has a dual appeal: the marvellous array of spring flowers in the churchyard and the story of the robins. A pair nested in the lectern 50 years ago and raised a family, an event recalled in carvings on the new lectern and on the porch gates. The original nest, in the old lectern, is still in the church.

Barnby   Map 4 ref K2
2 miles E of Beccles on the A146

Manager Wendy Pye puts out the welcome mat at the popular *Swan Inn*, which is located just off the A146 between Beccles and Lowestoft. It's very much the centre of village life, attracting both locals and tourists for anything from a convivial drink to a slap-up meal.

The pub area and the Fisherman's Cove restaurant are filled to the gunwales with nautical articles and artefacts (note the boat in the ceiling!) and the menu majors on fresh fish from local suppliers. The restaurant is particularly popular at weekends, so it's best to book a table for dinner. There are other good reasons for visiting Barnby, among them a garden centre, a riding school, a snail farm

The Swan Inn

and the church of St John the Baptist, dating from around 1200 and containing some notable wall paintings. What you might *not* see is the ghost of Black Shuck, a retriever who is said to haunt the local roads at night. *The Swan Inn, Swan Lane, Barnby, Suffolk, NR34 7QE. Tel: 01502 476646*

Mutford
Map 4 ref K2

4 miles E of Beccles off the A146

Beulah Hall is a country caravan park (non-residential) run by Carol and Peter Stanley. It's a delightful, quiet spot three miles from

Beulah Hall Caravan Park

the sea at Mutford, midway between Beccles and Lowestoft, and caters for campers as well as caravaners. The site is sheltered and secluded, in a conservation area abundant with wildlife, and visitors are welcome to bring their dogs at no extra charge. Carol breeds and shows Newfoundland dogs and has won best of breed at Cruft's. The hall is a favourite base for touring and for bird-watching; Minsmere RSPB sanctuary is a short drive away, and among other local attractions are the wildlife park at Kessingland, Banham Zoo with its monkey house, the otter trust at Bungay, and a couple of golf courses. On-site facilities include electrical connection, toilets, showers and free use of a heated outdoor swimming pool.

The owners make a deliberate, and successful, attempt to steer away from commercial aspects and the result is a quiet, civilised haven that attracts quiet, civilised people. *Beulah Hall, Dairy Lane, Mutford, Near Beccles, Suffolk, NR34 7QJ. Tel: 01502 476609*

Lowestoft

The most easterly town in Britain had its heyday as a major fishing port during the late 19th and early 20th centuries, when it was a mighty rival to Great Yarmouth in the herring fishing industry. That industry has been in major decline since World War I but Lowestoft is still a fishing port, and the trawlers still chug into the harbour in the early morning with the catches of the night. Guided tours of the **fish market** and the **harbour** are available. Tel: 01502 523000/ 730514.

Lowestoft is also a popular holiday resort, the star attraction being the lovely South Beach with its golden sands, safe swimming, two piers and all the expected seaside amusement and entertainment. *Claremont Pier*, over 600 feet in length, was built in 1902, ready to receive day trippers on the famous *Belle* steamers. The buildings in this part of town were developed in mid-Victorian times by the company of Sir Samuel Morton Peto, also responsible for Nelson's Column, the statues in the Houses of Parliament, the Reform Club and Somerleyton Hall, about which more anon.

Flying Fifteens, named after a class of racing boat designed by Uffa Fox, overlooks the beach and the sea, which inspired the tasteful decor and china. Diana and Peter Knight have created a high-quality tea room and gift shop where the excellent waitress service, quality of tea (over 20 varieties) and cleanliness have ensured continued membership of the National Tea Council's Guild of Tea Shops. Visitors can relax indoors or sit in the colourful lawned garden watching the world go by.

Diana bakes a variety of cakes and scones, among which Adnams Suffolk Ale boozy fruit cake and strawberry scones are particularly popular. The menu includes home-made soups, sandwiches, baguettes and omelettes. Beers and wine are also available.

Peter's gift shop is home to the work of local craft people, hand-crafted ceramics, unusual pieces and colourful items from around the world. Open 10.30 to 5 (excluding Monday) from June to

Flying Fifteens

September and some weekends out of season. High chairs available. No smoking indoors. *Flying Fifteens, 19a The Esplanade, Lowestoft, Suffolk, NR33 0QG. Tel: 01502 581188*

At the heart of the town is the old harbour, home to the **Royal Norfolk & Suffolk Yacht Club** and the **lifeboat station**. Further upriver is the commercial part of the port, used chiefly by ships carrying grain and timber. The history of Lowestoft is naturally tied up with the sea, and much of that history is recorded in fascinating detail in the **Lowestoft & East Suffolk Maritime Museum** (Tel: 01502 561963) with model boats, fishing gear, a lifeboat cockpit, paintings and shipwrights' tools. The setting is a flint-built fisherman's cottage in Sparrow's Nest Gardens. The **Royal Naval Patrol Museum** nearby remembers the minesweeping service in models, photographs, documents and uniforms (Tel: 01502 586250).

Lowestoft had England's first lighthouse, installed in 1609. The present one dates from 1874. Also in Sparrow's Nest Gardens is the **War Memorial Museum**, dedicated to those who served in World War II. There's a photographic collection of the bombing of the town, aircraft models and a chapel of remembrance (Tel: 01502 517950).

St Margaret's Church, notable for its decorated ceiling and copper-covered spire, is a memorial to seafarers, and the north aisle has panels recording the names of fishermen lost at sea from 1865 to 1923.

Lowestoft has some interesting literary and musical connections. The Elizabethan playwright, poet and pamphleteer, Thomas Nash(e), was born here in 1567. His last work, *Lenten Stuffe*, was a eulogy to the herring trade and specifically Great Yarmouth. Joseph Conrad (Jozef Teodor Konrad Korzeniowski), working as a deckhand on a British freighter bound for Constantinople, jumped ship here in 1878, speaking only a few words of the language in which he was to become one of the modern masters. Benjamin Britten, the greatest English composer of the 20th century, is associated with several places in Suffolk, but Lowestoft has the earliest claim, for it is here that he was born in 1913.

Just north of town with access from the B1385, **Pleasurewood Hill** is the largest theme park in East Anglia.

Oulton Broad, on the western edge of Lowestoft, is a major centre of amusement afloat, with boats for hire and cruises on the Waveney. It also attracts visitors to Nicholas Everitt Park to look around **Lowestoft Museum** (Tel: 01502 511457), housed in historic Broad House. Opened by The Queen and Prince Philip in 1985, the museum displays archaeological finds from local sites, some now lost to the sea, costumes, toys, domestic bygones, and a fine collection of Lowestoft porcelain. (The porcelain industry lasted from about 1760 to 1800, using clay from the nearby Gunton Hall Estate. The soft-paste ware, resembling Bow porcelain, was usually decorated in white and blue.)

Another museum, the **ISCA Maritime Museum**, has a unique collection of ethnic working boats, including coracles, gondolas, junks, dhows, sampans and proas.

Around Lowestoft

Carlton Colville
Map 4 ref K2

3 miles SW of Lowestoft on the B1384

Many an old bus-spotter has shed a nostalgic tear at the **East Anglia Transport Museum**, where children and ex-children climb aboard to enjoy rides on buses, trams and trolleybuses (one of the resident trolleybuses was built at the Garrett works in Leiston). The East Suffolk narrow-gauge railway winds its way around the site, and there's a 1930s' street with all the authentic accessories, plus lorries, vans and steamrollers. If you think it's far too long since

East Anglia Transport Museum

you saw a tram or trolleybus, this is the place for you. Open most days Easter to September (Tel: 01502 518459).

If the Transport Museum is heaven on earth to trolleybus buffs, then the local paradise for gardeners is *Early Dawn Nurseries & Garden Centre*. Just outside the village on the road to Mutford,

Early Dawn Nurseries and Garden Centre

it's run by a friendly family fivesome - Peter and Dawn Gissing, two daughters and a son - who put down their roots here 15 years ago. A leisurely stroll around the centre reveals plenty of things for sale in addition to almost every sort of flower and plant you can think of. There are pumps for rockery pools, garden tools and fencing, sundials with brass pedestals, gargoyles, stone pagoda lanterns, bird houses, Malaysian pots, garden furniture and barbecues. Open 8-5.30 (Sunday 10.30-4.30). *Early Dawn Nurseries & Garden Centre, Rushmere Road, Carlton Colville, Near Lowestoft, Suffolk, NR33 8HA. Tel: 01502 476340*

Also in Carlton Colville is the 15th century Church of St Peter, which incorporated parts of other buildings when restored in the 19th century.

Carlton Marshes is Oulton Broad's nature reserve with grazing marsh and fen, reached by the Waveney Way footpath. (Tel: 01502 564250 – also the number for the Suffolk Wildlife Trust.)

Blundeston
Map 4 ref K1
4 miles N of Lowestoft off the A12

Known chiefly as the village used by Charles Dickens as the birthplace of that writer's 'favourite child', David Copperfield. The morning light shining on the sundial of the church – which has the tallest, narrowest Saxon round tower of any in East Anglia – greeted young David as he looked out of his bedroom window in the nearby Rookery. He said of the churchyard: *"There is nothing half so green that I know anywhere, as the grass of that churchyard, nothing half so shady as its trees; nothing half so quiet as its tombstones."*

Blundeston has another notable literary connection: Blundeston Lodge was once the home of Norton Nichols, whose friend the poet Gray is reputed to have taken his inspiration for *An Elegy Written in a Country Church Yard* while staying there.

Neil and Niki Jermy, a friendly husband-and-wife team, have built up **Holly Garden Nurseries** from a small market garden into a considerable (and still expanding) nursery business which attracts visitors of all ages from far and wide. There's plenty of parking space and ample room to wander among the raised brick enclosures with their impressive range of flowers, plants and

Holly Garden Nurseries

shrubs. In an adjacent covered area are anything from pots to ornamental fountains - just about everything for the gardening
enthusiast. Cyclamen is something of a speciality, particularly at
Christmas time. *Holly Garden Nurseries, Flixton Road, Blundeston,
Near Lowestoft, Suffolk, NR32 5PL. Tel: 01502 730648*

Lound   Map 4 ref K1

5 miles N of Lowestoft off the A12

Lound's parish **Church of St John the Baptist**, in the very north
of the county, is sometimes known as the *'golden church'*. This epi-
thet is the result of the handiwork of designer/architect Sir Ninian
Comper, seen most memorably in the gilded organ-case with two
trumpeting angels, the font cover and the rood screen. The last is a
very elaborate affair, with several heraldic arms displayed. The surprise package here is the modern St Christopher mural on the north
wall. It includes Sir Ninian at the wheel of his Rolls Royce, and, in
1976, an aeroplane was added!

The Village Maid enjoys a picturesque rural setting by the pond
in Lound, a hamlet off the A12 a few miles north of Lowestoft. John
and Lisa Barnard-Richardson, recent arrivals from Berkshire, have
quickly made their mark here, and "The Maid" is popular with both
locals and tourists - booking is recommended, especially between
Thursday and Sunday. The building has been sympathetically renovated and wooden beams, bare brick walls, old wooden furniture
and log-burning fires create a cosy, old-world atmosphere. Period

The Village Maid

photographs of the village and villagers, dried flowers and a collection of teapots add to the charm. The owners provide a range of menus to suit all appetites, from super made-to-order sandwiches to multi-course meals. Fresh local produce is used whenever possible (fish is a speciality) and there are always several vegetarian options. Families are actively encouraged, and there are ducks and donkeys to keep the children amused. *The Village Maid, 71 The Street, Lound, Near Lowestoft, Suffolk, NR32 5LP. Tel: 01502 730441*

Somerleyton

Map 4 ref K1

5 miles NW of Lowestoft on the B1074

Somerleyton Hall, one of the grandest and most distinctive of stately homes, is a splendid Victorian mansion built in Anglo-Italian style by Samuel Morton Peto. Its lavish architectural features are complemented by fine state rooms, magnificent wood carvings (some by Grinling Gibbons) and notable paintings. The grounds include a renowned yew-hedge maze, where people have been going round in circles since 1846, walled and sunken gardens and a 300-foot pergola. There's also a sweet little miniature railway, and **Fritton Lake Countryworld**, part of the Somerleyton Estate, is a 10-minute drive away. The Hall is open to the public on most days in summer. For details call 01502 730224.

Samuel Morton Peto learned his skills as a civil engineer and businessman from his uncle and was still a young man when he put the Reform Club and Nelson's Column into his cv. The Somerleyton Hall he bought in 1843 was a Tudor and Jacobean mansion. He and his architect virtually rebuilt the place, and also built Somerleyton village, a cluster of thatched redbrick cottages. Nor was this the limit of Peto's achievements, for he ran a company which laid railways all over the world and was a Liberal MP, first for Norwich, then for Finsbury and finally for Bristol. His company foundered in 1863 and Somerleyton Hall was sold to Sir Francis Crossley, one of three brothers who made a fortune in mass-producing carpets. Crossley's son became Baron Somerleyton in 1916, and the Baron's grandson is the present Lord Somerleyton.

Dove Wood is an Edwardian end-of-terrace cottage set in attractive gardens close to the River Waveney, with broadland views and woodland walks. Lowestoft and the Broads are within easy reach, and it's an ideal base for sailing, rambling and bird-watching. It's also near the railway station, with trains to Norwich. Accommodation (all non-smoking) comprises a family room on the ground floor and a double and two singles on the first floor. The upstairs rooms can be let as a holiday flat on a self-catering basis.

Dove Wood

Campers (on request) can set up tents in the garden and, for a modest charge, use the indoor facilities.

Owner Hazel M Spencer also offers a boarding kennel and professional art tuition. Open all year round except at Christmas and New Year. Dove Wood does not provide an evening meal, but a pub serving food throughout the day is a short walk away. *Dove Wood Cottage, 5 Station Cottages, Somerleyton, Near Lowestoft, Suffolk, NR32 5QN. Tel: 01502 732627*

Herringfleet
Map 4 ref K1

5 miles NW of Lowestoft on the B1074

Standing above the River Waveney, the parish Church of St Margaret is a charming sight with its Saxon round tower, thatched roof and lovely glass. **Herringfleet Windmill** is a beautiful black-tarred smock mill in working order, the last survivor of the Broadland wind pump, whose job was to assist in draining the marshes. This example was built in 1820 and worked regularly until the 1950s. It contains a fireplace and a wooden bench, providing a modi-

Herringfleet Mill

cum of comfort for a millman on a cold night shift. To arrange a visit call 01473 583352.

Kessingland

Map 4 ref L2

3 miles S of Lowestoft off the A12

A small resort with a big history. Palaeolithic and Neolithic remains have come to light, and traces of an ancient forest have been unearthed on the sea bed. At the time of William the Conqueror, Kessingland prospered with its herring industry and was a major fishing port rivalled only by Dunwich. The estuary gradually silted up, sealing off the river with a shingle bank and cutting off the major source of wealth. The tower of the Church of St Edmund reaches up almost 100 feet – not unusual on the coast, where it provides a conspicuous landmark for sailors and fishermen. Most of the maritime trappings have disappeared: the lighthouse on the cliffs was scrapped 100 years ago, the lifeboat lasted until 1936 (having saved 144 lives), and there were several coastguard stations, one of them bought as a holiday home by the writer Rider Haggard.

Londoner Jill Thurston welcomes visitors from both home and abroad to her guest house **The Knoll**, which stands near the church in three acres of land secluded by trees and bushes. The garden is a delightful spot for sitting and relaxing, and beyond the grounds are extensive areas of farmland. The sea is not far away, and a bridle path runs by the house, linking the village with the coast and affording a particularly scenic walk. The four bedrooms are bright and airy, with double beds in pine and other furniture to match.

The Knoll

Breakfast is served in a hall which also includes a well-stocked bar and a fish tank. Jill keeps her horses in a paddock next to the house. No pets. *The Knoll, 182 Church Road, Kessingland, Near Lowestoft, Suffok, NR33 7SG. Tel: 01502 740354*

The major tourist attraction is the **Suffolk Wildlife Park**, 100 acres of coastal parkland that are home to a wide range of wild animals, from aardvarks to zebras by way of bats, flamingos, giraffes, meerkats and sitatunga. The flamingos have their own enclosure. The park has been home to several film stars, including two chimps who appeared in *Gorillas in the Mist* and Joey, leading player in the PG Tips TV commercials. Burmese pythons are used for snake-handling sessions – an attraction that's definitely not for everyone!

Covehithe   Map 4 ref K3
7 miles S of Lowestoft off the A12
Leave the A12 at Wrentham and head for the tiny coastal village of Covehithe which is remarkable for its 'church within a church'. The massive **Church of St Andrew**, partly funded by the Benedictine monks at Cluniac, was left to decline after being laid waste by Dowsing's men. The villagers could not afford a replacement on the same grand scale so in 1672 it was decided to remove the roof and sell off some of the material. From what was left a small new church was built within the old walls. The original tower still stands, spared by Cromwell for use as a landmark for sailors.

Southwold

A town full of character, and full of interest for the holidaymaker and for the historian. Though one of the most popular resorts on the east coast, Southwold has very little of the kiss-me-quick commercialism that spoils so many seaside towns. It's practically an island, bounded by creeks and marshes, the River Blyth and the North Sea, and has managed to retain the atmosphere of the last century. There are some attractive buildings, from pink-washed cottages to elegant Georgian town houses, many of them ranged around a series of greens which were left undeveloped to act as firebreaks after much of the town was lost in the great fire of 1659.

In a seaside town whose buildings present a wide variety of styles, shapes and sizes, William Denny's **Buckenham House** is among the most elegant and interesting. On the face of it a classic Georgian town house, it's actually much older, dating probably from the

Buckenham House

middle of the 16th century. Richard Buckenham, a wealthy Tudor merchant, was the man who had it built and it was truly impressive in size, as can be deduced from the dimensions of the cellar (now the Coffee House). Many fine features survive, including moulded cornices, carefully restored sash windows, Tudor brickwork and heavy timbers in the ceilings.

Since Buckenham's day it has seen service as a vicarage, a gentleman's club, offices and galleries, and today's Buckenham House fulfils a variety of roles, among them art gallery, art shop and gift shop. For the inner man the main attraction is undoubtedly the Coffee House, whose logo (a coffee pot filling a cup) is based on that of a London coffee house of around 1700; the Us in Buckenham and House are printed as Vs, another authentic sign of the times. The menu of coffees, teas and snacks both sweet and savoury offers a novel theory about the origin of the habit of tipping: users of coffee houses put money in a box marked T.I.P. (To Insure Promptness). Tips here are totally at the customer's discretion. *Buckenham House, 81 High Street, Southwold, Suffolk, IP18 6DS. Tel: 01502 722002*

The town, which was granted its charter by Henry VII in 1489, once prospered, like many of its neighbours, through herring fishing, and the few remaining fishermen share the harbour on the River Blyth with pleasure craft.Also adding to the period atmosphere is the pier, though as a result of storm damage this is much shorter than in the days when steamers from London called in on their way up the east coast.

Southwold first became favoured as an elegant, civilised holiday resort in Victorian times, and some of the quality and atmosphere of those days lives on at Christina Henshaw's ***Northcliffe Guest House***. It is one of several handsome Victorian houses that stand proudly on the promenade, within yards of the beach, yet a short, pleasant walk from the town centre with its fine selection of shops, pubs, restaurants and coffee houses. You may even see the horse-drawn drays! With its relaxed atmosphere, Northcliffe offers individually designed rooms, most with en suite facilities and sea views. One of the doubles has an interconnecting door with a single to provide compact though convenient family accommodation. The lounge, which also has sea views, is ideal for settling down with a good book or drink; a log fire keeps the chill at bay on colder days. Splendid home-cooked meals – two or three courses – and ample breakfasts are served in the licensed dining room. Indeed Northcliffe provides hotel facilities within an intimate guest house setting and is 'Highly Commended' by the English

Northcliffe Guest House

Tourist Board. Children and well-behaved dogs are welcome at all times. Turn right at the seafront end of Pier Avenue and you'll find Northcliffe about 200 yards along on the right. *Northcliffe Guest House, 20 North Parade, Southwold, Suffolk, IP18 6LT. Tel: 01502 724074*

There are also bathing huts, and a brilliant white lighthouse that's approaching its 100th birthday. It stands 100 feet tall and its light can be seen 17 miles out to sea. Beneath the lighthouse stands a little Victorian pub, the Sole Bay Inn, whose name recalls a battle fought off Southwold in 1672 between the British and French fleets and the Dutch. This was an episode in the Third Anglo-Dutch War, but why Sole Bay? Because the Duke of York, Lord High Admiral of England and later to be crowned James II, had taken Sutherland House in Southwold as his headquarters and it was from there that his fleet (along with the French) set sail. A distinguished victim of the battle was Edward Montagu, 1st Earl of Sandwich, great-grand-father of the man whose gambling mania did not allow him time for a formal meal. By inserting slices of meat between slices of bread, the 4th Earl ensured that his name would live on.

The Sole Bay Inn is one of several owned by the local brewery Adnams. One of the best known is the Lord Nelson, where traces can be seen of a smugglers' passageway leading to the cliffs. Where there were smugglers there are usually ghosts, and here it's a man in a frock coat who disappears into the cliff face. Adnams still use horse-drawn drays for local beer deliveries.

Southwold's maritime past is recorded in the **museum** set in a Dutch-style cottage in Victoria Street. Open daily in the summer, it records the famous battle and also local archaeology, geology and natural history, and the history of the Southwold railway. The Southwold Sailors' Reading Room contains pictures, ship models and other items, and at Gun Hill the Lifeboat Museum has a small collection of RNLI-related material with particular reference to Southwold. The main attraction at Gun Hill is a set of six 18-pounder guns, captured in 1746 at the Battle of Culloden and presented to the town (hitherto more or less undefended) by the Duke of Cumberland.

No visitor to Southwold should leave without spending some time in the splendid *Church of St Edmund King and Martyr*, which emerged relatively unscathed from the ravages of the Common-wealth. The lovely painted roof and wide screen are the chief glories, but the slim-stemmed 15th century pulpit and the Elizabethan Holy Table must also be seen. Outside the church, a splendid Jack o'the Clock – a little wooden man in War of the Roses armour – strikes his bell on the hour.

Around Southwold

Wangford
Map 4 ref K3

3 miles E of Southwold off the A12

There's some great walking in the country around Southwold, both along the coast and inland. At **Wangford**, a mile or so inland, **Henham Walks** are waymarked paths through Repton Park, lake and woods. A splendid place for a ramble or a picnic, or to see the wildlife, rare-breed sheep and Highland cattle. Also at Wangford is the Perpendicular Church of St Peter and St Paul, built on the site of a Benedictine priory. Even closer to Southwold is Reydon Wood Nature Reserve.

Anna and John Garwood's **Poplar Hall**, an extended 16th century thatched house in a lovely garden setting, offers luxury B&B accommodation in beautifully furnished rooms with beams, inglenooks and abundant character. There are three letting bedrooms, one en suite double and a double and a single (or small double) with private bathroom. John's profession as a consultant engineer

Poplar Hall

has taken him and Anna round the world, and the house is filled with intriguing mementoes and treasures from their travels - the puppets from Java are particularly delightful. Anna's skill as a potter is in evidence, too, and she is also responsible for all the drapes and curtains. Sumptuous breakfasts, with fish from Lowestoft, bacon from happy, hop-fed pigs, and home-made preserves, are served at a communal table in the dining room, from where guests can watch the activity at the bird-tables scattered around the garden. No smoking in the house. In addition to the B&B accommodation there are two self-catering cottages. The small hamlet of Frostenden Corner is about 3 miles from Southwold, starting on the B1127 Lowestoft road. *Poplar Hall, Frostenden Corner, Frostenden, Near Wangford, Suffolk, NR34 7JA. Tel: 01502 578549*

Blythburgh
Map 4 ref K4

3 miles E of Southwold, A1095 then A12

Blythburgh's **Church of Holy Trinity** is one of the wonders of Suffolk, a stirring sight as it rises from the reed beds, visible for miles around and floodlit at night to spectacular effect. This 'Cathedral of the Marshes' reflects the days when Blythburgh was a prosperous port with a bustling quayside wool trade. With the silting up of the river trade rapidly fell off and the church fell into decay. In 1577 the steeple of the 14th century tower was struck by lightning in a severe storm; it fell into the nave, shattering the font and taking two lives. The scorch marks visible to this day on the north door are said to be the claw marks of the Devil in the guise of hellhound Black Shuck, left as he sped towards Bungay to terrify the congregation of St Mary's.

Disaster struck again in 1644, when Dowsing and his men smashed windows, ornaments and statues, blasted the wooden angels in the roof with hundreds of bullets and used the nave as a stable, with tethering rings screwed into the pillars of the nave. Luckily, the bench-end carvings escaped the desecration, not being labelled idolatrous. These depict the Labours of the Months, and the Seven Deadly Sins. Blythburgh also has a Jack o'the Clock, a brother of the figure at Southwold, and the priest's chamber over the south porch has been lovingly restored complete with an altar made with wood from *HMS Victory*. The angels may have survived, but the font was defaced to remove the signs of the sacraments.

This marvellous ecclesiastical treasure house is what brings most visitors to Blythburgh, but the wonderful countryside also has its attractions. A mile south, at the junction of the A12 and the Walberswick road, ***Toby's Walks*** is an ideal place for a picnic and, like so many places in Suffolk, has its own ghost story. This concerns Tobias Gill, a dragoon drummer who murdered a local girl and was hanged here after a trial at Ipswich. His ghost is said to haunt the heath, but this should not deter picnickers.

The **Norman Gwatkin Nature Reserve** is an area of marsh and fen with two hides, walkways and a willow coppice.

Wenhaston
Map 4 ref J4

5 miles E of Southwold off the A12

The **Church of St Peter** cannot compete as a spectacle with Blythburgh's Holy Trinity, but is well worth a detour. Saxon stones are embedded in its walls but the most remarkable feature is the doom (Last Judgement), said to have been painted around 1500 by a monk from Blythburgh.

Margaret Plues owns and runs **The Compasses Inn**, which stands in this sleepy village, just off the A12 near Southwold, that boasts no fewer than five commons and an ancient church with a notable Doom painting on wooden panels. The surrounding area is great walking country, and the pub's regulars include the occupants of local caravan sites and holiday cottages. There's easy off-street parking, and a colourful garden in which Margaret plans to offer cream teas on Summer Sunday afternoons.

The small popular bistro (open evenings, with lunches by arrangement) offers a standard menu of local fish, steaks and cutlets, with several vegetarian options. Special dishes, such as paella and curries, are available with notice and theme evenings are held regularly. The Compasses can accommodate guests in three characterful bedrooms whose furnishings include chairs made from barrels.

The Compasses Inn

Breakfasts are as large as you like and can be taken quite late - a perfect place to relax and unwind. Children are not allowed but the owners are particularly fond of dogs - there are pictures of them all over the place - and pets are welcome in all rooms. *The Compasses Inn, The Street, Wenhaston, Suffolk, IP19 9EF. Tel: 01502 478319*

Walberswick

Map 4 ref K4

1 miles SW of Southwold on the B1387

The story is familiar: flourishing fishing port; grand church; changing of the coastline due to erosion and silting; decline of fishing and trading; no money to maintain the church; church falls into disrepair. Towards the end of the 16th century, a smaller church was built within the original St Andrew's, by then in ruins through neglect. The situation in Walberswick had been exacerbated by the seizing of church lands and revenues by the king, and by a severe fire.

Fishing hardly exists today, and boating in Walberswick is almost entirely a weekend and holiday activity. The tiny 'church within a church' is still in use, its churchyard a nature reserve. South of the village is the bird sanctuary of **Walberswick & Westleton heaths**. Walberswick has, for two centuries, been a magnet for painters, the religious ruins, the beach and the sea being favourite subject for visiting artists. The tradition continues unabated, and many Academicians have made their homes here.

The 600-year-old **Bell Inn** stands near the village green just moments from the beach and the harbour. To the north, across the

The Bell Inn

estuary of the River Blyth, lies Southwold, to the south Dunwich and Minsmere bird sanctuary, to the west the marvellous church at Blythburgh. Inside the Bell there's a splendidly old-fashioned look, with low beamed ceilings, floors worn with age, open log fires and an assortment of high-backed settles, chairs and tables in lots of little alcoves.

When the weather is kind the garden is the place to be, sitting under a parasol and enjoying the sea views. Indoors or out, there's excellent eating to be had, with all the traditional pub fare and more, from sandwiches and salads to fish and chips, scampi and chili. Fish and shellfish feature strongly among the blackboard specials, and there are always several vegetarian options and a mouthwatering selection of sweets. The other side of this enormously appealing inn is accommodation, comprising six comfortably appointed bedrooms, all with private facilities. A warm welcome and a comfortable stay are assured by landlady Sue Ireland-Cutting. *The Bell Inn, Ferry Road, Walberswick, Southwold, Suffolk, IP18 6TN. Tel: 01502 723109*

CHAPTER FIVE
Southeast Suffolk

Tide Mill, Woodbridge

Chapter 5 - Area Covered

For precise location of places please refer to the colour maps found at the rear of the book.

5
Southeast Suffolk

Introduction

The sea brings its own dangers and also brings them in human form, and it was against the threat of a Napoleonic invasion that Martello Towers were built, in the tradition of Saxon and Tudor forts and precursors of concrete pillboxes. The name of the towers comes from Cape Martella in Corsica, when such a tower resisted for some time a stout cannonade in 1794, and on the Duke of York's recommendation the tower was adapted for use in England. Starting just before the end of the 18th century, over 100 of these sturdy circular fortified towers were built along the coast from Suffolk to Sussex. Aldeburgh's at Slaughden is the most northerly (and the largest), the tower at Shoreham in Sussex the southernmost. They are generally around 30 feet in height, with immensely thick walls on the seaward side, and surrounded by a moat. Entry was usually by bridge or ladder on the land side. They were never needed for their original purpose, and now stand as a picturesque oddity along the shore.

The marshes by the coast have traditionally been a source of reeds, the raw material for the thatch that is such a pretty sight on so many Suffolk buildings. Thatch covered the majority of buildings in medieval times, but fear of fire made thatching less popular in the 19th century, and tiles or slates (both also much easier to construct) became the standard material for roofing. Many of the reed beds were drained and given over to grazing, but the threat of invasion caused many to be reflooded in World War II. This action brought about the renaissance of the reed beds and with it a lifeline to many threatened bird species. The wartime emergency measure led to an increased demand for thatch, and the beds are carefully managed to bring about the best balance between the quality of the crop and the well-being of the wildlife. Reed cutting happens between December and February, the beds being drained in preparation and reflooded after the crop has been gathered. Thatching itself is a highly skilled craft, but 10 weeks of work can give a thatched roof 50 years of life. Organised walks of the reed beds take place from time to time – wellies essential.

Along the Coast

Dunwich *Map 4 ref K4*
4 miles SW of Southwold off the B1105

Surely the Hidden Place of all Hidden Places! Dunwich was once the capital of East Anglia, founded by the Burgundian Christian missionary St Felix and for several centuries a major trading port (wool and grain out; wine, timber and cloth in) and a centre of fishing and shipbuilding. The records show that in 1241 no fewer than 80 ships were built for the king. By the middle of the next century the best days were over as the sea attacked from the east and a vast bank of sand and shingle silted up the harbour. The course of the river was diverted, the town was cut off from the sea and the town's trade was effectively dead. For the next 700 years, the relentless forces of nature continued to take their toll, and all that remains now of ancient Dunwich are the ruins of a Norman leper hospital, the archways of a medieval friary and a buttress of one of the nine churches which once served the community.

Today's village comprises a 19th century church and a row of Victorian cottages, one of which houses the **Dunwich museum**. Local residents set up the museum in 1972 to tell the Dunwich story; the historical section has displays and exhibits from Roman, Saxon and medieval times, the centrepiece being a large model of the town at its 12th century peak. There are also sections for natural history, social history and the arts. Experts have calculated that the main part of old Dunwich extended up to seven miles beyond its present boundaries, and the vengeance of the sea has thrown up inevitable stories of drama and mystery. The locals say that when a storm is threatening, the sound of submerged church bells can still be heard tolling under the waves as they shift in the current. Other tales tell of strange lights in the ruined priory and the eerie chanting of long-gone monks.

Dunwich Priory

Dunwich Forest, immediately inland from the village, is one of three – the others are further south at Tunstall and Rendlesham – named by the Forestry Commission as Aldewood Forest. Work started on these in 1920 with the planting of Scots pine, Corsican pine and some Douglas fir; oak and poplar were tried but did not thrive in the sandy soil. The three forests, which between them cover nearly 9,000 acres, were almost completely devastated in the hurricane of October 1987, Rendlesham alone losing more than a million trees, and the replanting will take many years to restore them.

South of the village lies **Dunwich Heath**, one of Suffolk's most important conservation areas, comprising the beach, splendid heather, a field study centre, a public hide, and an information centre and restaurant in converted coastguard cottages. 1998 marks the 30th anniversary of the heath being in the care of the National Trust.

Around Dunwich Heath are the attractive villages of Westleton, Middleton, Theberton and Eastbridge.

Run by Ralph and Joanne Major and their families, **The Eels Foot Inn** is a delightful find in a quiet location north of Leiston, near the sea and Minsmere bird sanctuary. It was originally three cottages, dating from about 1700; one of them was occupied by the village cobbler, hence the name - eels foot is part of a cobbler's last. Four acres of grounds include a huge garden with wooden furniture

The Eels Foot Inn

and swings, and there are great views across the meadows and reed beds. The bars and eating area have a simple rustic look, with bare walls and floors, exposed beams and sturdy wooden furniture. Food is served every lunchtime and evening except Monday evening and runs from ploughman's platters, savoury pies and ham, egg and chips to strawberry sundae and treacle pud. Overnight accommodation is available in a single low-ceilinged bedroom with bathroom en suite. The inn also offers parking space and toilet facilities for caravaners and campers. *The Eels Foot Inn, Eastbridge, Near Leiston, Suffolk, IP16 4SN. Tel: 01728 830154*

In **Westleton**, the 14th century thatched Church of St Peter, built by the monks of Sibton Abbey, has twice seen the collapse of its tower. The first fell down in a hurricane in 1776 and its smaller wooden replacement collapsed when a bomb fell in World War II. The village is the main route of access to the RSPB-managed **Minsmere Bird Sanctuary**, the most important sanctuary for wading birds in eastern England. The marshland was flooded during World War II, and nature and this wartime emergency measure created the perfect habitat for innumerable birds. More than 100 species nest here, and a similar number visit. It's a birdwatcher's paradise, with many hides, and the **Suffolk Coastal Path** runs along the foreshore.

A little way inland from Westleton lies **Darsham**, where another nature reserve is home to many varieties of birds and flowers.

Theberton   *Map 3 ref J5*
12 miles S of Southwold on the B1122

A one-time working farm half a mile from the B1122 Leiston-Yoxford road is where Janet Baxter runs her excellent B&B business. *The Alders*, a period pinkwashed building, was formerly two farm cottages, and much of its original charm and character survives. The

The Alders

three letting bedrooms are comfortable and well appointed, and the views delightful. Minsmere Bird Reserve and Snape Maltings are within easy reach. Janet's splendid English breakfasts, with free-range eggs, bacon from the local butcher and home-made marmalade and jam, get the day under way in fine style. The house is a little out of the way, so be sure to get directions from Janet when booking. *The Alders, Potter Street, Theberton, Near Leiston, Suffolk, IP16 4RL. Tel: 01728 831790*

Yoxford   *Map 4 ref J5*
10 miles SW of Southwold on the A12

Once an important stop on the London-Yarmouth coaching route, Yoxford now attracts visitors with its pink-washed cottages and its arts and crafts, antique and food shops. Look for the cast-iron signpost outside the church, with hands pointing to London, Yarmouth and Framlingham set high enough to be seen by the driver of a stagecoach.

The Griffin is a country inn with a restaurant, four letting rooms and a long and interesting history. Some of that history includes a spell as the local manor and the restaurant area has recently been refurbished to reveal original beams and walls. Windows have been added to create plenty of light, and scrubbed wooden tables complete the period picture. The menu includes local venison sausages and several dishes based on medieval recipes. The bedrooms (two doubles, a twin and a single), all with super little bathrooms making the best use of the limited space, have also been done out in

The Griffin Inn

sympathy with the surroundings. Landlord Ian Terry and friends entertain with 'music, songs and werse' using period and modern instruments, and there are regular jazz/blues nights, special events and a popular Thursday quiz. Don't worry about the ghost - he's as rare a sight as the smugglers who haunted the place in the 18th century. *The Griffin Inn, High Street, Yoxford, Suffolk, IP17 3EP. Tel: 01728 668229*

Sibton

Map 4 ref I4

12 miles SW of Southwold on the A1120

Two miles west of Yoxford, on the A1120, Sibton is known chiefly for its abbey (only the ruins remain), the only Cistercian house in Suffolk. The Church of St Peter is certainly not a ruin and should be seen for its fine hammerbeam and collar roof.

Park Farm is a 60-acre arable farm and in the square-set Georgian-fronted farmhouse Margaret Gray offers bed and breakfast accommodation with the option of an evening meal. There are three bedrooms, two twins with en suite facilities and a double with a private bathroom next door. Beautiful quilts, hand-made by the owner, grace the beds and also serve as tapestry-style wall hangings in the old-fashioned dining room, where a large oval antique

Park Farm

table is complemented by an inviting chaise longue. As we went to press work was in progress on transforming outbuildings into three luxurious self-catering apartments, each with all mod cons including facilities for disabled guests. An adjacent games room will double as premises for craft courses – with quilting a speciality. The surrounding countryside is a delight for nature-lovers, ramblers or anyone needing a good dose of rural peace, and with the sea only a short drive away, this is a perfect spot for a holiday. *Park Farm, Sibton, Saxmundham, Suffolk, IP17 2LZ. Tel: 01728 668324*

Saxmundham
Map 4 ref J5
12 miles SW of Southwold off the A12
A pretty name for a little town that was granted its market charter in 1272. On the font of the church is the carving of a woodwose, a tree spirit or green man – he, and others like him, have given their name to a large number of pubs, in Suffolk and elsewhere. The only thing in ruins in Sax is the bus garage!

A warm and enthusiastic welcome awaits every visitor to **The White Hart**, a high-street hostelry run by Jackie and Keith Webber with the help of their daughters Tracy and Nicola. Behind the traditional facade - white-painted brick, shuttered upper windows, unusual pepperpot chimneys - the scene in the bars is exactly what you would expect, with heavy oak furniture, wood panelling, log fires, English water colours and photographs of old Sax. The surprise item is a

The White Hart

collection of drumsticks, souvenirs of the various groups who come to play here on a Saturday night. The back of the building opens on to the car park and a colourful beer garden. This is a great place for downing a convivial pint, and even better if you stay for a meal. Everything on the blackboard menu is home-made, portions are exceedingly generous, and the sight and smell of the food being prepared will stir even the most sluggish of gastric juices. Good wine list, too. For overnight stays there are five bedrooms sharing two bathrooms. *The White Hart, 18 High Street, Saxmundham, Suffolk, IP17 1DB. Tel: 01728 602009*

The comments in the visitors book rightly praise the civilised sur-roundings and the obliging personal service offered at **Kiln Farm**. Penton Lewis's B&B is a real home from home, with lovely old paint-ings, carefully chosen ornaments and soothing classical music striking just the right note. The house is situated in Benhall just off the A12, west of Saxmundham, and a short drive from Snape; it

Kiln Farm

often attracts festival musicians. Three double bedrooms provide everything needed for a comfortable stay, and breakfast is taken either in the dining room or out on the patio. There are extensive gardens on all sides, with lawns, apple trees, rose bushes and privet hedges. Children and dogs are welcome. Get directions when book-ing as Benhall is not on all maps. *Kiln Farm, Benhall, Saxmundham, Suffolk, IP17 1HA. Tel: 01728 603166*

Around Saxmundham

Bruisyard   *Map 4 ref I5*
4 miles NW of Saxmundham off the B1119
Just west of the village is the **Bruisyard Vineyard, Winery and Herb Centre**, a complex of a 10-acre vineyard with 13,000 Müller Thurgau grape vines, a wine-production centre, herb and water gardens, a tea shop and a picnic site.

Peasenhall   Map 4 ref I4
6 miles NW of Saxmundham on the A1120

A little stream runs along the side of the main street, whose buildings present several styles and ages. Most distinguished is the old timbered **Woolhall**, splendidly restored to its 15th century grandeur. The oddest is certainly a hall in the style of a Swiss chalet, built for his workers by James Josiah Smyth, grandson of the founder of James Smyth & Sons. This company, renowned for its agricultural drills, was for more than two centuries the dominant industrial presence in Peasenhall. On the south side of St Michael's churchyard stands the 1805 drill mill where James Smyth manufactured his Nonpareil seed drills, one of which is on display in Stowmarket's museum.

Leiston   Map 4 ref J5
4 miles E of Saxmundham off the B1119

The first **Leiston Abbey** was built on Nunsmere marshes in 1182 but in 1363 the Earl of Suffolk rebuilt it on its present site. It became one of the largest and most prestigious monasteries in the country, and its wealth probably spelt its ruin, as it fell within Henry VIII's plan for the dissolution of the monasteries. A new abbey was built by the ruins of the old, and the restored old hall is used as a base for a group of young musicians.

For 200 years the biggest name in Leiston was that of Richard Garrett, who founded an engineering works here in 1778 after starting business in Woodbridge. In the early years ploughs, threshers, seed drills and other agricultural machinery were the main products, but the company later started one of the country's first production lines for steam machines. The Garrett works are now the **Long Shop Museum**, the factory buildings having been lovingly restored, and many of the Garrett machines are now on display, including traction engines, a steam-driven tractor and a road roller. There's also a section where the history and workings of steam engines are explained. A small area of the museum recalls the USAAF's 357th fighter group, who flew from an airfield outside Leiston during World War II. One of their number, a Captain Chuck Yeager, was the first man to fly at more than the speed of sound

The Garrett works closed in 1980 and what could have been a disastrous unemployment situation was to some extent alleviated by the nuclear power station at **Sizewell**. The coast road in the centre of Leiston leads to this establishment, where visitors can take tours, on foot with access to buildings at Sizewell A or by minibus, with guide and videos, round the newer PWR Sizewell B.

Aldringham
4 miles E of Saxmundham on the B1122

Map 4 ref J6

The village church is notable for its superb 15th century font, and the village inn was once a haunt of smugglers. It now helps to refresh the visitors who flock to the **Aldringham Craft Market**, founded in 1958 and extending over three galleries, with a serious selection of arts and crafts, clothes and gifts, pottery, basketry, books and cards.

Thorpeness
6 miles E of Saxmundham on the B1353

Map 4 ref K6

A unique holiday village with mock-Tudor houses and the general look of a series of eccentric film sets. Buying a considerable pocket

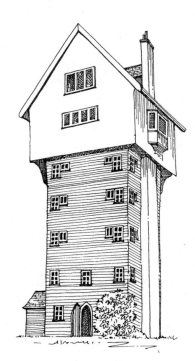

The House in the Clouds

of land called the Sizewell estate in 1910, the architect, barrister and playwright Glencairn Stuart Ogilvie created what he hoped would be a fashionable resort with cottages, some larger houses and a shallow boating and pleasure lake called the Meare. The 85' water tower, built to aid in the lake's construction, looked out of place, so Ogilvie disguised it as a house, known ever since as the House in the Clouds, and now available for rent as a holiday home. The neighbouring mill, moved lock, stock and millstones from Aldringham, stopped pumping in 1940 but has been restored and now houses a visitor centre. Every August, in the week following the Aldeburgh Carnival, a regatta is held on the Meare, culminating in a splendid fireworks show. Thorpeness is very much a one-off, not at all typical Suffolk, but with a droll charm that is all its own.

After a walk round the fascinating sights of Thorpeness or a leisurely row on the lake, the **Meare Shop & Tea Room** is the place to head for. All the rowers have to do is disembark, as the tea room is literally on the edge of the Meare. Teas, cakes and light snacks are served, and when the sun shines there are plenty of outside seats. The shop in the same premises keeps a stock of books, postcards, gifts and seaside essentials. Owners Christopher and Elizabeth Everett also run Tulip Cottage, just a few steps away.

The Meare Shop and Tea Room

This is a modern three-storey house with a steeply raked boat-shaped roof that's very appropriate for the setting. The building, which has recently been renovated, provides overnight accommodation in three double bedrooms and one single. Balconies on the first-floor rooms overlook the Meare, while rear rooms enjoy direct views out to sea. A very popular place to pause in this most extraordinary holiday village. *The Meare Shop & Tea Room and Tulip Cottage, Aldeburgh Road, Thorpeness, Near Leiston, Suffolk, IP16 4NW. Tel: 01728 452156*

Aldeburgh   *Map 4 ref K6*
6 miles SE of Saxmundham on the A1094
And so down the coast road to Aldeburgh, another of those coastal towns that once prospered as a port with major fishing and ship-building industries. Drake's *Greyhound* and *Pelican* were built at Slaughden, now taken by the sea, and during the 16th century some 1,500 people were engaged in fishing. Both industries declined as shipbuilding moved elsewhere and the fishing boats became too large

to be hauled up the shingle. Suffolk's best-known poet, George Crabbe, was born at Slaughden in 1754 and lived in the poor times. He clearly reflected the melancholy of those days when he wrote of his fellow townsmen:

"Here joyless roam a wild amphibious race,
With sullen woe displayed in every face;
Who far from civil arts and social fly,
And scowl at strangers with suspicious eye."

He was equally evocative concerning the sea and the river, and the following lines written about the River Alde could apply to several others in the county:

"With ceaseless motion comes and goes the tide
Flowing, it fills the channel vast and wide;
Then back to sea, with strong majestic sweep
It rolls, in ebb yet terrible and deep;
Here samphire-banks and salt-wort bound the flood
There stakes and seaweed withering on the mud;
And higher up, a ridge of all things base,
Which some strong tide has rolled upon the place."

Crabbe it was who created the character of the solitary fisherman Peter Grimes, later the subject of an opera composed by another Aldeburgh resident, Benjamin Britten.

Aldeburgh's role gradually changed into that of a holiday resort, and the Marquess of Salisbury, visiting early in the 19th century, was one of the first to be attracted by the idea of sea-bathing without the crowds. By the middle of the century the grand houses that had sprung up were joined by smaller residences, the railway arrived, a handsome water tower was put up (1860) and Aldeburgh prospered once more. There were even plans for a pier, and construction started in 1878, but the project proved too difficult or too expensive and was halted, the rusting girders being removed some time later.

One of the town's major benefactors was Newson Garrett, a wealthy businessman who was the first mayor under the charter of the Local Government Act of 1875. This colourful character also developed the **Maltings at Snape**, but is perhaps best remembered through his remarkable daughter Elizabeth, who was the first woman doctor in England (having qualified in Paris at a time when women could not qualify here) and the first woman mayor (of Aldeburgh, in 1908). This lady married the shipowner James Skelton Anderson, who established the golf club in 1884.

If the poet were alive today he would have a rather less crabbed opinion of his fellows, especially at carnival time on a Monday in August, when the town celebrates with a colourful procession of floats and pedestrians, a fireworks display and numerous other social events.

As for the arts, there is, of course, the **Aldeburgh Festival**, started in 1948 by Britten and others; the festival's main venue is Snape Maltings, but many performances take place in Aldeburgh itself.

The maritime connection remains very strong. There has been a lifeboat here since 1851 and down the years many acts of great heroism are recorded. The very modern lifeboat station is one of the town's chief attractions for visitors, and there are regular practice launches from the shingle beach. A handful of fishermen still put out to sea from the beach, selling their catch from their little wooden huts, while down at Slaughden a thriving yacht club is the base for sailing on the Orde and sometimes on the sea. At the very southern tip of the town the Martello tower serves as a reminder of the power of the sea: old pictures show it standing well back from the waves, but now the seaward side of the moat has disappeared and the shingle is constantly being shored up to protect it. Beyond it a long strip of marsh and shingle stretches right down to the mouth of the river at Shingle Street.

Back in town, there are several interesting buildings, notably the **Moot Hall** and the parish **Church of St Peter and St Paul**. Moot Hall is a 16th century timber-framed building that once apparently stood in the centre of town. It hasn't moved, but the sea long ago took away several houses and streets. Inside the hall is a museum of town history and finds from the nearby Snape burial ship. Britten set the first scene of *Peter Grimes* in the Moot Hall. A sundial on the south face of the hall proclaims, in Latin, that it only tells the time when the sun shines.

The church, which stands above the town as a very visible landmark for mariners, contains a memorial to George Crabbe and a beautiful stained-glass window, the work of John Piper, depicting three Britten parables for church performance, *Curlew River, The Burning Fiery Furnace* and *The Prodigal Son*. Britten is buried in the churchyard, part of which is set aside for the benefit of wildlife.

Aldeburgh has a number of good hotels and fine restaurants specialising in locally-caught fish and shellfish.

Friston
Map 4 ref J6
3 miles SE of Saxmundham off the A1094
The tallest post mill in England is a prominent sight on the Aldeburgh-Snape road, moved from Woodbridge in 1812, just after its construction. It worked by wind until 1956, then by engine until 1972. St Mary's Church dates from the 11th century.

Snape
Map 4 ref J6
3 miles S of Saxmundham on the A1094
The "boggy place" has a long and interesting history, and in 1862 an Anglo-Saxon ship was discovered. Since that time regular finds have been made, with some remarkable cases of almost perfect preservation. Snape, like Aldeburgh, benefited from the philanthropy of the Garrett family, one of whose members built the primary school and set up the **Maltings**, centre of the **Aldeburgh Music Festival**.

The last 30 years have seen the development of the **Snape Maltings Riverside Centre**, a group of shops and galleries that offers a unique shopping experience. The site is a complex of restored Victorian granaries and malthouses that is also the setting for the renowned Aldeburgh festival.

The Maltings began their designated task in the 1840s and con-

The Snape Maltings Riverside Centre

tinued thus until 1965, when the pressure of modern techniques brought them to a halt. There was a real risk of the buildings being demolished but George Gooderham, a local farmer, bought the site to expand his animal feeds business and soon saw the potential of the redundant buildings (his son Jonathan is the current owner of the site, Julia Pipe the Director of Retailing).

The concert hall came first, in 1967, and in 1971 the Craft Shop was established as the first conversion of the old buildings for retailing. Conversion and expansion continue to this day, and in the numerous stylish outlets visitors can buy anything from fudge to country-style clothing, from herbs to household furniture, from silver buttons to top hats. Plants and garden accessories are also sold, and art galleries feature the work of local painters, potters and sculptors. The centre hosts regular painting, craft and decorative art courses, and the latest expansion saw the creation of an impressive country-style department store.

Shoppers, even in these splendid surroundings, need the occasional break for light refreshment, and here they can head for the Plough & Sail pub (serving lunches and evening meals) or the Granary Tea Shop selling cakes and savouries made on the premises. River trips in summer leave from Snape and cruise up to the ancient Iken church. The centre is located on the B1069, just south of Snape village, and clearly signposted from the A12 (A1094). *Snape Maltings Riverside Centre, Snape, Near Saxmundham, Suffolk, IP17 1SR. Tel: 01728 688303/5*

A short distance west of Snape, off the B1069, lies Blaxhall, slightly famous for its growing stone. *The Blaxhall Stone*, which lies in the yard of Stone Farm, is reputed to have grown to its present size (5 tons) from a comparative pebble, the size of a football, when it first came to local attention 100 years ago. Blaxhall getting mixed up with 'Blarney'?

Campsea Ashe   Map 3 ref I6
6 miles NE of Woodbridge on the B1078

On towards Wickham Market, the road passes through Campsea Ashe in the parish of Campsey Ashe. The 14th century Church of St John the Baptist has an interesting brass showing a 14th century rector in full priestly garb.

The Old Rectory, a spacious Georgian house next to the church, offers one of Suffolk's most agreeable experiences of fine dining and civilised country-house living. Four acres of gardens afford tranquillity and splendid views, and shrubs and rhododendrons screen

The Old Rectory

the house from the road. Stewart Bassett is a genial character who greets guests with an eccentric charm and proposes a no-choice three-course meal in consultation with diners. His cooking is exceptional, relying on the best, freshest produce, and a meal here has the feel of a high-class dinner party. The old-style dining rooms with log fires are used in winter, while the wicker-furnished conservatory comes into its own in summer. A distinguished wine list complements the splendid cooking, and Stewart does the rounds of the tables towards the end of dinner. Up the handsome staircase are eight beautifully furnished bedrooms, each with its own style and character. They include two four-posters, a Victorian room and an Attic room. No smoking in the dining rooms or bedrooms. No dinner on Sunday. *The Old Rectory, Campsea Ashe, Near Woodbridge, Suffolk, IP13 0PU. Tel: 01728 746524*

The Talbot is a 'proper' country pub in a quiet village. Built in 1880, with later additions, it was recently totally renovated by owner Brian Foster and his partner Cally, and their presence and choice of interior decor provide bags of atmosphere and plenty of interest. Most notable is a fascinating collection of early American weapons, and there are also some saddles and some unusual stringed instruments. Brian was involved in the Cambridge Folk Festival and they both play the instruments. The locals play cribbage and darts. Large bay windows look out across the lane and over to the fields, and white picket fencing surrounds the garden, where chairs and tables

The Talbot

are set out in the summer. No food is served here, but this is beer territory and there's a good choice of real and cask ales, some produced by small local brewers. Well-behaved children and well-behaved dos are welcome. The pub sign depicts front and rear views of a talbot, a large hunting dog which is now extinct. *The Talbot, Station Road, Campsea Ashe, Near Woodbridge, Suffolk, IP13 0PT. Tel: 01728 748439*

Wickham Market
Map 4 ref I6
5 miles N of Woodbridge off the A12
Places to see in this straggling village are a picturesque watermill by the River Deben and All Saints Church, whose 137' octagonal tower has a little roof to shelter the bell. At Boulge, a couple of miles southwest of Wickham Market, is the grave of Edward Fitzgerald, whose free translation of *The Rubaiyat of Omar Khayyam* is an English masterpiece. Tradition has it that on his grave is a rose bush grown from one on Omar Khayyam's grave in Iran. More of 'Old Fitz' in Woodbridge.

Easton
Map 4 ref I6
5 miles N of Woodbridge off the B1078
A scenic drive leads to the lovely village of Easton, one of the most colourful, flower-bedecked places in the county. A remarkable sight to the west of the village is the 2-mile-long **crinkle-crankle** wall that surrounds Easton Park. This extraordinary type of wall, also

known as a ribbon wall, wavers snake-like in and out and is much stronger than if it were straight. This particular wall, said to be the world's longest, was built by lord of the manor the Earl of Rochford in the 1820s. The manor house is not open to the public.

Tucked away three miles off the A12 in the beautiful Deben valley, *Easton Park Farm* is one of Suffolk's greatest attractions. 1998 sees its 25th year, and in that time more than a million visitors have passed through the gates to have a great day out and to leave knowing a lot more about the ways of the countryside than when they arrived. It's a marvellous place to bring the family, as the children can have endless fun feeding and making friends with the little animals in Pets Paddock, riding ponies or simply running around in the adventure playground.

The showpiece of the park is the Victorian dairy, an ornate octagonal building, while the Dairy Centre is contrastingly modern, with walkways over the top of the stalls and a viewing gallery over the milking parlour. Many

Easton Park Farm

breeds of farm animals – some now rare – enjoy a happy and protected life at Easton, including White Park, Longhorn and Red Poll cows, Jacob and Suffolk sheep, black-headed Bagot goats and the wonderful Suffolk heavy horses. In the forge, a resident blacksmith is busy at work most days, maintaining the vintage farm machinery and making horseshoes and gifts for sale. The Green Trail is a delightful walk leading to the River Deben and home to a wide variety of plants and birds and insects. Exercise and fresh air generate thirsts and appetites, both of which will be satisfied in the Stables Tea Room. The park is open mid-March to end-September except Mondays other than Bank Holidays and Mondays in July/August. *Easton Park Farm, Easton, Near Wickham Market, Suffolk, IP13 0EQ. Tel: 01728 746475*

The public house next-door to the church is **The White Horse**, a charming 16th century building in Suffolk pink, with a steeply raked tiled roof, tall chimneys and ecclesiastical leaded windows. Pip Smith, born in the village, returned to run this hub of the community and with his wife Sally has created the warmest and most welcoming of settings. Sally is responsible for the hanging baskets that adorn the house and outbuildings and for the lovely tiered garden, where Huey

The White Horse

the goat does sterling service as a lawnmower. Sally also does all the cooking, catering for families, cricket teams, ravenous ramblers and a loyal band of regulars from as far afield as Southend. Savoury pies and bakes, curries and all-day breakfasts are among the favourite orders. The inside of the pub is just as appealing as the outside, with open fires, Welsh dressers showcasing splendid old plates, bare wooden tables, open fires, flagstones and numerous cosy corners. A fascinating collection of pictures of the pub and village in 1919 adorns the walls. Live music Saturday evening. *The White Horse, The Street, Easton, Suffolk, IP13 0ED. Tel: 01728 746456*

Parham   *Map 4 ref I6*
8 miles N of Woodbridge on the B1116
Parham airfield is now agricultural land, but in the control tower

and a hut are memorabilia of the 390th Bomb Group of the USAAF.

Ufford   Map 4 ref I7
4 miles N of Woodbridge off the A12

Pride of place in a village that takes its name from Uffa (or Wuffa), the founder of the leading Anglo-Saxon dynasty, goes to the 13th century *Church of the Assumption*. The font cover, which telescopes from 5 feet to 18 feet in height, is a masterpiece of craftsmanship, its elaborate carving crowned by a pelican. Many 15th century benches have survived but Dowsing smashed the organ and most of the stained glass – what's there now is mainly Victorian, some of it a copy of 15th century work at All Souls College, Oxford. Ufford is where the Suffolk Punch originated, Crisp's 404 being, in 1768, the progenitor of the breed.

Bredfield   Map 3 ref H7
3 miles N of Woodbridge off the A12

The funny thing about Bredfield is that sometimes nothing happens, and a plaque on the wall of the village pub actually records nothing at all happening on a day in 1742. On a day in 1809, however, something *did* happen: Edward Fitzgerald was born. Something else happened in 1953: a wrought-iron canopy with a golden crown, made at the village forge, was put on the crossroads pump to celebrate Queen Elizabeth II's coronation.

Woodbridge

Udebyge, Wiebryge, Wodebryge, Wudebrige … just some of the ways of spelling this splendid old market town since first recorded in 970. As to what it means, it could simply be 'wooden bridge' or 'bridge by the wood', but the most likely and most interesting explanation is that it is derived from Anglo-Saxon words meaning 'Woden's (or Odin's) town'.

Standing at the head of the Deben estuary, it is a place of considerable charm, with a wealth of handsome, often historic buildings and a considerable sense of history, as both a market town and a port.

The shipbuilding and allied industries flourished here as at most towns on the Suffolk coast, and it is recorded that both Edward III, in the 14th century, and Drake in the 16th sailed in Woodbridge ships. There's still plenty of activity on and by the river, though nowadays it is all leisure-oriented. The town's greatest benefactor was Thomas Seckford, who rebuilt the abbey, paid for the chapel in the north aisle of St Mary's Church and founded the original almshouses in Seckford Street. In 1575 he gave the town the splendid Shire Hall on Market Hill. Originally used as a corn exchange, it now houses the **Suffolk Horse Museum**, which is an exhibition devoted to the Suffolk Punch breed of heavy working horse, the oldest such breed in the world. The history of the breed and its rescue from near-extinction in the 1960s is covered in fascinating detail, and there's a section dealing with the other famous Suffolk breeds – the Red Poll cattle, the Suffolk sheep and the Large Black pigs. Opposite the Shire Hall is **Woodbridge Museum**, a treasure trove of information on the history of the town and its more notable residents, and from here it is a short stroll down the cobbled alleyway to the magnificent parish Church of St Mary, where Seckford was buried in 1587.

Seckford naturally features prominently in the museum, along with the painter Thomas Churchyard, the map-maker Isaac Johnson and the poet Edward Fitzgerald. 'Old Fitz' was something of an eccentric and, for the most part, fairly reclusive. He loved Woodbridge and particularly the River Deben, where he often sailed in his little boat *Scandal*.

Woodbridge is lucky enough to have two marvellous mills, both in working order, and both great attractions for the visitor. **The Tide Mill**, on the quayside close to the town centre, dates from the late

The Tide Mill and Quay

18th century (though the site was mentioned 600 years previously) and worked by the power of the tide until 1957. It has been meticulously restored and the waterwheel still turns, fed by a recently created pond which replaced the original huge mill pond when it was turned into a marina. ***Buttrum's Mill***, named after the last miller, is a tower mill standing just off the A12 by-pass a mile west of the town centre. She is a marvellous sight, and her six storeys make her the tallest surviving tower mill in Suffolk. There is a ground-floor display of the history and workings of the mill.

Many of the town's streets are traffic-free, so shopping is a real pleasure. If you should catch the Fitzgerald mood and feel like 'a jug of wine and a loaf of bread', Woodbridge can oblige with a good variety of pubs and restaurants.

Around Woodbridge

Melton
Map 3 ref I7

1 mile E of Woodbridge on the B1084

John and Bridgitte Walker's ***Horse & Groom*** is an imposing former coaching inn on the main street, with plenty of parking space and a walled garden. Many original features remain intact - huge wooden

beams, oak panelling, bare brick fireplace - and old bottles, pictures of old Melton, horse brasses and converted gas lamps complete the period scene. It's very much a pub that sells food, not a restaurant that sells beer, and regulars sit around the bar enjoying a chat in a comfortable, relaxed atmosphere. The eating part - Stables restaurant - comprises 18 covers, and a leisurely meal can be enjoyed either here or in the main bar (no children in that bar, but they're welcome everywhere else and a children's menu will be provided on request). Quick snacks are also available. Five twin bedrooms, comfortably

The Horse & Groom

furnished in pine, make this an ideal place for a stopover after a good meal with a glass or two of cask ale or reasonably priced wine. *The Horse & Groom, Yarmouth Road, Melton, Near Woodbridge, Suffolk, IP12 1QB. Tel: 01394 383566*

Eyke
Map 3 ref I7

3 miles NE of Woodbridge on the A1152

Brian and Jackie Edwards run **The Elephant & Castle**, which was built in 1650 as a private house and was converted to an inn as long ago as 1715. Behind its cheerful whitewashed facade it serves many purposes: watering hole for a lively local community, three letting bedrooms for bed and breakfast accommodation, provider of

The Elephant & Castle

good plain English meals and a meeting place for clubs in the neighbourhood (pony and trap, classic motorcycles). The inn has a central bar serving both sides at once, and the old bottle and jug area can still be seen. There are some interesting old pictures of the pub in its original state, plus postcards from around the world and line drawings (for sale) of local places of interest. Other assets are ample car parking space, a garden, and a caravan site with five pitches. If the social centre of Eyke's life is the Elephant & Castle, the spiritual centre is All Saints Church, dating back to 1150 and notable for some fine oak carvings of animals and birds. *The Elephant & Castle, Eyke, Near Woodbridge, Suffolk, IP12 2QG. Tel: 01394 460241*

A mile or so east of Woodbridge on the opposite bank of the Deben is the **Sutton Hoo burial site**, a group of a dozen grassy barrows which hit the headlines in 1939. Excavations brought to light the outline of an 80' long Anglo-Saxon ship, filled with one of the greatest hoards of treasure ever discovered in Britain. The priceless find includes gold coins and ornaments, silverware, weapons and armoury, drinking horns and leather cups; it is housed in the British Museum, but there are exhibitions, replicas and plenty of other interest at the site. Research continues, and it is now believed that the ship was the burial place of Raedwald, of the Wuffinga dynasty, who was King of East Anglia from about 610 to 625. Access to the site is on foot from the B1083.

Bromeswell
Map 3 ref I7

3 miles NE of Woodbridge off the B1084

A quiet village in a scenic setting. Bromeswell's church has a 12th century archway at its entrance, a 15th century font and an unusual Flemish well. The angels in the hammerbeam roof are plastic replicas of the originals, whose wings were clipped by Cromwell's men.

Rendlesham
Map 3 ref I7

5 miles NE of Woodbridge on the A1152

The **Church of St Gregory the Great** dates from the 14th century, but there is evidence (not physical, unfortunately) of an earlier Christian presence in the shape of Raedwald's palace.

Rendlesham Forest, part of the Forest of Aldewood, was ravaged by the great hurricane of October 1987 but seven years before that, on Christmas night 1980, another visitation had occurred. Security guards at RAF Woodbridge, at that time a front line NATO base, spotted strange lights in the forest and went to investigate. They came upon a 9 foot high triangular object with a series of lights around it. As they approached, it did what all good UFOs do and flew off before it could be photographed. The next day the guards returned to the spot where it had landed and found three depressions in the ground. The UFO was apparently sighted again two days later and security in the area was tightened. No explanation has ever been forthcoming about the incident, but interest in it continues and from time to time guided walks to the landing site are arranged.

Tunstall
Map 3 ref I6
8 miles NE of Woodbridge on the B1078

An excellent place to pause, with signposted walks along the forest drive, plenty of picnic areas and an interesting church to see. St Michael's retains some fine old box pews, a single brass and a memorial to the local residents who lost their lives in World War I.

Butley
Map 3 ref J7
5 miles NE of Woodbridge on the B1084

At the northern edge of Rendlesham Forest, the village has a splendid 14th century gatehouse, all that remains of **Butley Priory**, an Augustinian priory founded by Ranulf de Glanville in 1171. The gatehouse is, by itself, a fairly imposing building, with some interesting flintwork on the north facade (1320) and baronial carvings. Butley still has a working mill, remarkable for its fine Regency porch, and the parish church is Norman, with a 14th century tower.

There are some splendid country walks here, notably by **Staverton Thicks**, which has a deer park and woods of oak and holly. The oldest trees date back more than 400 years. Butley Clumps is an avenue of beech trees planted in clumps of four, with a pine tree at the centre of each clump – the technical term for such an arrangement is a quincunx. Butley was long renowned for its oysters, and the beds have recently been revived.

Chillesford
Map 3 ref J7
6 miles E of Woodbridge on the B1084

Brick was once big business here, and while digging for clay the locals made many finds, including hundreds of varieties of mollusc and the skeleton of an enormous whale. Chillesford supplies some of the clay for Aldeburgh brickworks.

Orford
Map 3 ref J7
12 miles E of Woodbridge at the end of the B1084

Without doubt one of the most charming and interesting of all the places in Suffolk, with something to please everyone. The ruins of one of the most important **castles** in medieval England are a most impressive sight, even though the keep is all that remains of the original building commissioned by Henry II in 1165. The walls of the keep are 10 feet deep, and behind them are many rooms and passages in a remarkable state of preservation. A climb up the spiral staircase to the top provides splendid views.

St Bartholomew's Church was built at the same time, though the present church dates from the 14th century. A wonderful sight at night when floodlit, the church is regularly used for the performance of concerts and recitals, and many of Benjamin Britten's works were first heard here. At the east end lie the still-splendid Norman remains, all that is left of the original chancel.

These two grand buildings indicate that Orford was a very important town at one time. Indeed it was once a thriving port, but the steadily growing shingle bank of **Orford Ness** gradually cut it off from the sea, and down the years its appeal has changed. The sea may have gone, but the river is still there, and in summer the quayside is alive with yachts and pleasure craft. On the other side of the river is Orford Ness, the largest vegetated shingle spit in England which is home to a variety of rare flora and fauna. The lighthouse marks the most easterly point in Britain (jointly with Lowestoft).

Access to the spit, which is in the hands of the National Trust, is by ferry from Orford quay only (Tel: 01394 450057). For many years the ness was out of bounds to the public, being used for various military purposes, including pre-war radar research under Sir Robert Watson-Watt. Boat trips also leave Orford quay for the RSPB reserve of **Havergate Island**, haunt of avocet and tern (the former returned in 1947 after being long absent).

Back in the market square are a handsome town hall, two pubs with a fair quota of smuggling tales, a well-loved restaurant serving Butley oysters and a smokehouse where kippers, salmon, trout, ham, sausages, chicken and even garlic are smoked over Suffolk oak.

Orford Crafts Shop is much more than its name suggests, and Stuart Bacon much more than a trader in local crafts. Certainly it's the hand-woven baskets that first take the eye, displayed in special frames in the old stables and in the

Orford Crafts Shop

main building, where visitors will also come across an amazing array of pottery and wooden collectibles stacked among the hessian and matting, lit by old oil lamps and accompanied by gentle classical music. The surprise lies in wait upstairs, where Stuart's other expertise is in Suffolk underwater studies, and students and researchers come here for detailed information on all aspects of the Suffolk coast, currently featuring Dunwich and a possible Armada wreck. *Orford Crafts Shop, Front Street, Orford, Suffolk, IP12 2LN. Tel: 01394 450678*

Bawdsey
Map 3 ref I8
7 miles SE of Woodbridge on the B1083
The B1083 runs from Woodbridge through farming country and several villages (Sutton, Shottisham, Alderton) to Bawdsey, beyond which lie the mouth of the River Deben, the end of the Sussex Coastal Path, and the ferry to Felixstowe. The late-Victorian Bawdsey Manor was taken over by the Government and became the centre for radar development when Orford Ness was deemed unsuitable. By the beginning of World War II there were two dozen secret radar stations in Britain and radar HQ moved to Dundee from Bawdsey. The manor is now a leisure centre.

Ramsholt
Map 3 ref I8
7 miles SE of Woodbridge off the B1083
Ramsholt is a tiny community on the north bank of the Deben a little way up from Bawdsey. The pub is a popular port of call for yachtsmen, and half a mile from the quay, in quiet isolation, stands the Church of All Saints with its round tower. Road access to Ramsholt is from the B1083 just south of Shottisham, which has an alternative claim to Hoxne as the place of Edmund's martydom.

Hollesley
Map 3 ref I8
5 miles SE of Woodbridge off the B1083
The Deben and the Ore turn this part of Suffolk almost into a peninsula and on the seaward side lie Hollesley and Shingle Street. The latter stands up on a shingle bank at the entrance to the Ore and comprises a row of little houses, a coastguard cottage and a Martello tower. Its very isolation is an attraction, and the sight of the sea rushing into and out of the river is worth the journey.

Brendan Behan did not enjoy his visit. Brought here on a swimming outing from the Borstal at Hollesley, he declared that the waves had *"no limit but the rim of the world"*. Looking out to the bleak North Sea, it is easy to see what he meant.

CHAPTER SIX
Ipswich and South Suffolk

The Guildhall, Lavenham

Chapter 6 - Area Covered

For precise location of places please refer to the colour maps found at the rear of the book.

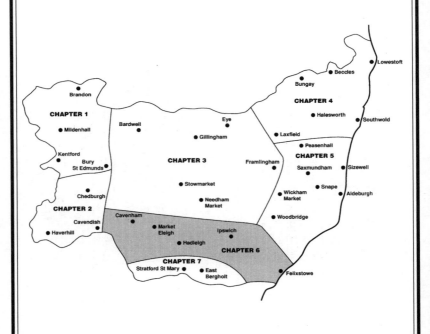

6
Ipswich & South Suffolk

Introduction

Much of Suffolk's character comes from its rivers, and in this part of the county the Orwell and the Stour mark the boundaries of the Shotley Peninsula. The countryside here is largely unspoilt, with wide-open spaces between scattered villages. The relative flatness of Suffolk gives every encouragement for motorists to leave their machines, and the peninsula, still relatively peaceful, is ideal for a spot of walking or cycling or boating ...

... or settling down with a good book. Writers have been inspired down the centuries to live among and write about the coasts and heath and forest, the villages and harbours and rolling farmland. Daniel Defoe, John Evelyn and William Cobbett all had nice things to say about Bury St Edmunds and Ipswich, and in the last century Algernon Swinburne and Henry James were impressed with the mystery of Dunwich. George Crabbe wrote lyrically about the poor times in Aldeburgh and Slaughden, while Edward Fitzgerald showed his love of Woodbridge and its river in his writings. Suffolk has often been used as a setting for novels, notably by Charles Dickens – here in fact, his characters in fiction; P D James, who found Dunwich and Minsmere suitably mysterious locations; Arthur Ransome, devoted to Pin Mill; Ruth Rendell/Barbara Vine, using several places in the county; Wilkie Collins, setting a splendid part of *No Name* in Aldeburgh; and Stevie Smith, some of whose *Novel in Yellow Paper* takes place in Felixstowe. Kathleen Hale came to Aldeburgh for a family holiday and used the town (she called it Owlbarrow) and many of its familiar landmarks in her story about Orlando the Marmalade Cat's seaside holiday. The cartoonist Giles lived near Ipswich and his immortal Grandma is remembered by a statue in Princes Street.

Ipswich

History highlights Ipswich as the birthplace of Cardinal Wolsey, but the story of Suffolk's county town starts very much earlier. It has been a port since the time of the Roman occupation and by the 7th century the Anglo-Saxons had expanded it into the largest port in the country. King John granted a civic charter in 1200, confirming

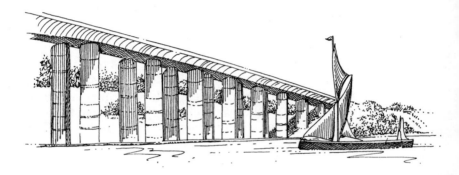

Orwell Bridge, Ipswich

the townspeople's right to their own laws and administration, and for several centuries the town prospered as a port exporting wool, textiles and agricultural products.

Thomas Wolsey arrived on the scene in 1475, the son of a wealthy butcher and grazier. Educated at Magdalen College, Oxford, he was ordained a priest in 1498 and rose quickly in influence, becoming chaplain to Henry VII and then Archbishop of York, a cardinal and Lord Chancellor under Henry VIII. He was quite indispensable to the king and had charge of foreign policy as well as powerful sway over judicial institutions. He also managed to amass enormous wealth, enabling him to found a grammar school in Ipswich and Cardinal's College (later Christ Church) in Oxford. Wolsey had long been hated by certain nobles for his low birth and arrogance, and they were easily able to turn Henry against him when his attempts to secure an annulment from the Pope of the king's marriage to

Corn Hill, Ipswich

Catherine of Aragon met with failure. Stripped of most of his offices following a charge of overstepping his authority as a legate, he was later charged with treason but died while travelling from York to London to face the king. His death put an end to his plans for the grammar school, and all that remains now is a red-brick gateway.

When the cloth market fell into decline in the 17th century a respite followed in the following century, when the town was a food distribution port during the Napoleonic Wars. At the beginning of the 19th century the risk from silting was becoming acute at a time when trade was improving and industries were springing up. The Wet Dock, constructed in 1842, solved the silting problem and, with the railway arriving shortly after, Ipswich could once more look forward to a safe future. The Victorians were responsible for considerable development and symbols of their civic pride include the handsome **Old Custom House** by the Wet Dock, the Town Hall and the splendid **Tolly Cobbold brewery**, rebuilt at the end of the 19th century, 150 years after brewing started on the site. Guided tours take visitors through the whole brewing process (Tel: 01473 231723). In Grimwade Street stands *Peter's Ice Cream Factory*, built 100 years ago. Guided tours take place several times a day, and there's a museum, restaurant and shop (Tel: 01473 253265). Victorian enterprise depleted the older buildings, but a number survive, notably the Tudor houses where Wolsey was born, the Ancient House with its wonderful pargeting, and a dozen medieval churches. St Margaret's is the finest of these, boasting some very splendid flintwork and a double hammerbeam roof.

Christchurch Mansion is a beautiful Tudor home standing in a 65-acre park. Furnished as an English country house, it contains a major collection of works by Constable and Gainsborough and many other paintings, prints and sculptures by Suffolk artists from the 17th century onwards. Tel: 01473 253246.

The town's main *museum* is in a Victorian building in the High Street. Displays include a natural history gallery, a wildlife gallery complete with a model of a mammoth, a reconstruction of a Roman villa and replicas of Sutton Hoo treasures. A recent addition is a display of elaborately carved timbers from the homes of wealthy 17th century merchants. Tel: 01473 213761

Mortimer's Seafood Restaurant, owned and run for the past 15 years by Kenneth Ambler, is a superb conversion of an old warehouse right on the waterfront of what is a mixture of marine and working dock. One part of the restaurant is light and airy, with a glass ceiling, the other darker, softer and more intimate. The decor is tastefully restrained, with old photographs of the warehouse and

the quay, watercolours by Thomas Mortimer, hanging plants and a few fishy things on the walls, The menu is all about seafood, and the chefs in their open-to-view kitchen prepare the catch in a generally straightforward

Mortimer's Seafood Restaurant

way that lets the freshness speak for itself. Some dishes are familiar favourites – grilled plaice with lemon and parsley butter, wing of skate with capers in a black butter sauce – while others, like chargrilled tuna with a Catalan-style tomato sauce, are a little out of the ordinary. Fish soup is a splendidly satisfying starter, oysters come as they are or grilled, and there's always a selection of marinated and smoked fish. Closed lunchtime Saturday and all Sunday. *Mortimer's Seafood Restaurant, Wherry Quay, Ipswich, Suffolk, IP4 1AS. Tel: 01473 230225*

In a former trolleybus depot on Cobham Road is the **Ipswich Transport Museum**, a fascinating collection of vehicles, from prams to fire engines, all made or used around Ipswich.

Managed by a go-ahead young couple, Steve and Tereska McAllister, **The Black Horse** is a whitewashed building with distinctive tall chimneys and a steeply raked tiled roof. Though not far from the main attractions of metropolitan Ipswich, it enjoys a secluded location surrounded by trees, with a church on either side and one of the town's oldest buildings just behind.

The Black Horse

Before the town expanded it was definitely a country pub, standing in meadows leading down to the River Gipping. It was reputedly once a smugglers' pub - the usual tales abound - and nautical bric-a-brac shares shelf space with an extaensive collection of old bottles. Brick-faced walls and bare wooden ceilings supported by oak beams assist the traditional look along with old-fashioned furnishings and an amazing old brick fireplace that's an integral part of the bar area. With its chatty, relaxed atmosphere, The Black Horse appeals to a wide cross-section of locals and visitors and is particularly popular with families on a summer outing, with a large open area providing plenty of space for running around or taking the sun. Food is served from 11am to 10pm (noon-9.30 on Sunday). *The Black Horse, Black Horse Lane, Ipswich, Suffolk, IP1 2EF. Tel: 01473 214741*

On the outskirts of town, signposted from Nacton Road, is **Orwell Country Park**, a 150-acre site of wood, heath and reedbeds by the Orwell estuary. At this point the river is crossed by the imposing Orwell Bridge, a graceful construction in pre-stressed concrete that was completed in 1982 and is not far short of a mile in length.

Notables from the world of the arts with Ipswich connections include Thomas Gainsborough, who got his first major commissions here to paint portraits of local people; David Garrick, the renowned actor-manager, who made his debut here in 1741 as Aboan in Thomas Southerne's *Oroonoko*; and the peripatetic Charles Dickens, who stayed at the Great White Horse while still a young reporter with the *Morning Chronicle*. Soon afterwards, he featured the tavern in *The Pickwick Papers* as the place where Mr Pickwick wanders inadvertently into a lady's bedroom. Sir V S Pritchett was born in Ipswich, while Enid Blyton trained as a kindergarten teacher at Ipswich High School.

Southeast of Ipswich

The peninsula created by the River Deben and the River Orwell is one of the prettiest areas in Suffolk, its winding lanes leading through a delightful series of quiet rural villages and colourful riverside communities. In medieval times it enjoyed very little of the affluence that came from the wool trade and one man above all was responsible for its eventual development. That man was Colonel George Tomline, who at one time owned almost all the area and who virtually 'invented' Felixstowe.

Nacton   *Map 3 ref H8*
4 miles SE of Ipswich off the A14

South of Nacton's medieval church lies **Orwell Park House**, which was built in the 18th century by Admiral Edward Vernon, sometime

Member of Parliament for Ipswich. The admiral, who had won an important victory over the Spanish in the War of Jenkins Ear, was know to his men as Old Grog, because of his habit of wearing a cloak of coarse grogram cloth. His nickname passed into the language when he ordered that the rum ration dished out daily to sailors should be diluted with water to combat the drunkenness that was rife in the service. That was in 1740, and a ration of 'grog' was officially issued to sailors until 1970.

George Tomline bought the splendid house in 1857 and made it even more splendid, adding a conservatory, a ballroom and towers. He also changed the facade to handsome Georgian. The house became the setting for some of the grandest shooting parties ever seen in this part of the world, and such was the power of the Tomlines that they were able to move the village away from the house to its present site.

Nacton picnic site in Shore Lane (signposted from the village) commands wonderful views of the Orwell and is a prime spot in winter for birdwatchers. The birds feed very well off the mud flats.

Levington   *Map 3 ref H8*
5 miles SE of Ipswich off the A14
A pretty village on the banks of the Orwell. Fisons established a factory here in 1956, and developed the now famous Levington Compost. On the foreshore below the village is an extensive marina which has brought an extra bustle to the area. The coastal footpath along the bank of the Orwell leads across the nature reserve of ***Trimley Marshes*** and on to Felixstowe.

Trimley St Mary & Trimley St Martin   *Map 3 ref H9*
6 miles SE of Ipswich off the A14
Twin villages with two churches in the same churchyard. The Cavendish family were famous Trimley residents, their best known member being the adventurer Thomas Cavendish. In 1590 he became the second man to sail round the world and two years later he died on another voyage. He is depicted on the village sign.

Trimley Marshes were created from farmland and comprise grazing marsh, reed beds and wetland that's home to an abundance of interesting plant life and many species of wildfowl, waders and migrant birds. Access is on foot from Trimley St Mary.

Newbourne   *Map 3 ref H8*
7 miles E of Ipswich off the A12
A small miracle occurred here on the night of the hurricane of Octo-

ber 1987. One wall of the ancient St Mary's Church was blown out and with it the stained glass, which shattered into fragments. One piece, showing the face of Christ, was found undamaged and was later incorporated into the rebuilt wall. Two remarkable inhabitants of Newbourne were the Page brothers, who both stood over 7 feet tall; they enjoyed a career touring the fairs and are buried in Newbourne churchyard.

Waldringfield   *Map 3 ref I8*
7 miles E of Ipswich off the A12
Waldringfield lies on a particularly beautiful stretch of the Deben estuary, and the waterfront is largely given over to leisure boating and cruising. The quay was once busy with barges, many of them laden with coprolite. This fossilised dung, the forerunner of fertilizer, was found in great abundance in and around Waldringfield, and a number of exhausted pits can still be seen.

Felixstowe   *Map 3 ref I9*
12 miles SE of Ipswich off the A14
Until the early 17th century Felixstowe was a little known village of no great importance, but it was the good Colonel Tomline of Orwell Park who put it on the map by creating a port to rival its near neighbour Harwich. He also started work on the Ipswich-Felixstowe railway (with a stop at Nacton for the grand parties), and 1887 saw the completion of both projects. Tomline also developed the resort aspects of Felixstowe, rivalling the amenities of Dovercourt, and when he died in 1887 most of his dreams had become reality. (He was, incidentally, cremated, one of the first in the county to be so disposed of in the modern era.) What he didn't live to see was the pier, opened in 1904 and still in use.

The town has suffered a number of ups and downs this century, but on the run-up to the Millennium thrives as one of England's busiest ports, having been much extended in the 1960s. The resort is strung out round a wide, gently curving bay, where the long seafront road is prettified by trim lawns and gardens.

The Martello tower is a noted landmark, as is the ***pier,*** which was once long enough to merit an electric tramway. It was shortened as a security measure in World War II. All the usual attractions are provided for the holidaymaker, and a very unusual one. This is the ***Felixstowe Water Clock***, a curious piece assembled from dozens of industrial bits and pieces.

The original fishing hamlet from which the Victorian resort was developed lies beyond a golf course north of the town. This is

Felixstowe Ferry, a cluster of holiday homes, an inn, a boatyard, fishing sheds and a Martello tower. The sailing club is involved mainly with dinghy racing and the whole place becomes a hive of activity during the class meetings. A ferry takes foot passengers (plus bicycles) across to Bawdsey and back into Chapter 5.

At the southernmost tip of the peninsula is **Landguard Point**, where a nature reserve supports rare plants and migrating birds.

Just north on this shingle bank is **Landguard Fort**, built in 1718 (replacing an earlier construction) to protect Harwich harbour and now home to **Felixstowe Museum**. The museum is actually housed in the Ravelin Block (1878), which was used as a mine storage depot by the army when a mine barrier was laid across the Orwell in World War I. A fascinating variety of exhibits includes local history, model aircraft and model paddle steamers, Roman coins and the history of the fort itself, which was the scene of the last invasion of English soil, by the Dutch in 1667. Beyond the fort is an excellent viewing point for watching the comings and goings of the ships.

South of Ipswich

Freston
Map 2 ref G8
3 miles S of Ipswich off the B1080

An ancient village on the south bank of the Orwell, worth visiting for some fine old buildings and some curiosities. The most curious and best known of these buildings is the six-storey Tudor tower by the river in **Freston Park** (it's actually best viewed from across the river). The red-brick house, built around 1570, has just six rooms, one per storey. It might be a folly, but it was probably put up as a lookout tower to warn of enemies sailing up the river. The nicest theory is that it was built for Ellen, daughter of Lord Freston, to study a different subject each day, progressing floor by floor up the tower (and with Sundays off, presumably). A 4,000-year-old archaeological site at Freston was revealed by aerial photography.

Woolverstone
Map 2 ref G9
4 miles S of Ipswich on the B1456

Dating back to the Bronze Age, Woolverstone has a large marina along the banks of the Orwell. One of the buildings in the complex is **Cat House**, where it is said that a stuffed white cat placed in the window would be an all-clear sign for smugglers. Woolverstone House was originally St Peter's Home for *'Fallen Women'*, run by nuns. It was designed by Sir Edwin Lutyens and has its own chapel and bell tower.

Tattingstone

Map 2 ref G9

4 miles S of Ipswich off the A137

Tattingstone Wonder, on the road between Tattingstone and Stutton, looks like a church from the front, but it isn't! It was built by a local landowner to provide accommodation for estate workers. He presumably preferred to look at a church from his mansion than some plain little cottages. Tattingstone lies at the western edge of Alton Water, a vast man-made lake created as a reservoir in the late 1970s. A footpath runs round the perimeter, and there's a wildlife sanctuary. On the water itself all sorts of leisure activities are on offer, including angling, sailing and windsurfing.

Stutton

Map 2 ref G9

6 miles S of Ipswich on the B1080

The elongated village of Stutton lies on the southern edge of the reservoir. The Domesday Book records six manor houses standing here, and there are still some grand properties down by the Stour. St Peter's Church stands isolated overlooking Holbrook Bay, and a footpath from the church leads all the way along the river to Shotley Gate. A little way north, on the B1080, Holbrook is a large village with a brook at the bottom of the hill. Water from the brook powered Alton Mill, a weather-boarded edifice on a site occupied by watermills for more than 900 years. The mill is now a restaurant.

Chelmondiston

Map 3 ref H9

5 miles S of Ipswich on the B1456

The church here is modern, but incorporates some parts of the original, which was destroyed by a flying bomb in 1944.

In the same parish is the tiny riverside community of **Pin Mill**, a well-known beauty spot and sailing centre. The river views are particularly lovely at this point, and it's also a favourite place for woodland and heathland walks. Pin Mill was once a major manufacturer of barges, and those imposing craft can still be seen, sharing the river with sailing boats and pleasure craft. Each year veteran barges gather for a race that starts here at Buttermans Bay and ends at Harwich. Arthur Ransome, author of *Swallows and Amazons*, stayed here and had boats built. His *We Didn't Mean To Go To Sea* starts aboard a yacht mooring here.

The local hostelry is the 17th century Butt & Oyster, much visited, much painted and one of the best known pubs in the county. To the east of the Quay is Cliff Plantation, an ancient coppice wood of alder and oak.

Erwarton
Map 3 ref H9
6 miles S of Ipswich off the B1456

An impressive red-brick Jacobean gatehouse with a rounded arch, buttresses and pinnacles is part of **Erwarton Hall**, the family home of the Calthorpes. Anne Boleyn was the niece of Philip Calthorpe and visited as a child and as queen. Just before her execution Anne apparently requested that her heart be buried in the family vault at St Mary's Church. A casket in the shape of a heart was found there in 1836 and when opened contained dust. It was resealed and laid in the Lady Chapel.

Shotley
Map 3 ref H9
8 miles S of Ipswich on the B1456

Right at the end of the peninsula, with the Orwell on one side and the Stour on the other, Shotley is best known as the home of *HMS Ganges*, where generations of sailors received their training. The main feature is the 142' mast up which trainees would shin at the passing-out ceremony. A small museum records the history of the establishment from 1905 to 1976, when it became a policy academy. At the very tip is a large marina where a classic boat festival is an annual occasion.

West of Ipswich

Hintlesham
Map 2 ref F8
7 miles W of Ipswich on the A1071

Hintlesham's glory is a magnificent hall dating from the 1570s, when it was the home of the Timperley family. It was considerably altered during the 18th century, when it acquired its splendid Georgian facade. For some years the hall was owned by the celebrated chef Robert Carrier, who developed it into the county's leading restaurant. It still functions as a high-class hotel and restaurant.

Hadleigh
Map 2 ref F8
10 miles W of Ipswich on the A1071

Old and not-so-old blend harmoniously in a variety of architectural styles. Timber-framed buildings, often with elaborate plasterwork, stand in the long main street as a reminder of the prosperity generated by the wool trade in the 14th to 16th centuries, and there are also some fine houses from the Regency and Victorian periods. The 15th century **Guildhall** with two overhanging storeys, the Deanery Tower and the church are a magnificent trio of huge appeal and contrasting construction – timber for the Guildhall, brick for the tower and flint for the church.

Guthrun, the Danish leader who was captured by Alfred and pardoned on condition that he became a Christian, made Hadleigh his HQ and lived here for 12 years. He was buried in the church, then a wooden construction but later twice rebuilt. In the south chapel of the present church is a 14th century bench-end carving depicting the scene of the wolf guarding the head of St Edmund. The wolf is wearing a monk's habit, indicating a satirical sense of humour in the carpenter. Also of interest is the **clock bell**, which stands outside the tower. A famous resident of Hadleigh was the rector Dr Rowland Taylor, who was burnt at the stake on Aldham Common for refusing to hold a mass. A large stone, inscribed and dated 1555, marks the spot.

There are two good walks from Hadleigh, the first being along the Brett with access over medieval **Toppesfield Bridge**. The other is a walk along the disused railway line between Hadleigh and Raydon through peaceful, picturesque countryside. At Raydon a few buildings survive from the wartime base of the 353rd, 357th and 358th Fighter Groups of the USAAF.

Two miles east of Hadleigh is **Wolves Wood**, an RSPB reserve with woodland nature trails and no wolves.

Kersey   Map 2 ref E8
12 miles W of Ipswich off the A1141

The ultimate Suffolk picture-postcard village, a wonderful collection of timbered merchants' houses and weavers' cottages with paint and thatch. The main street has a **water splash**, which, along with the 700-year-old Bell Inn, has featured in many films and travelogues. The Church of St Mary, which overlooks the village from its hilltop position, is of massive proportions, testimony to the wealth that came with the wool and cloth industry. Kersey's speciality was a coarse twill broadcloth much favoured for greatcoats and army uniforms. Headless angels and mutilated carvings are reminders of the Puritans' visit to the church, though some treasures survive, including the ornate flintwork of the 15th century south porch. Traditional craftsmanship can still be seen in practice at the Kersey Pottery, which sells many items of stoneware plus paintings by Suffolk artists.

Chelsworth   *Map 2 ref E7*
14 miles W of Ipswich off the A1141

An unspoilt delight in the lovely valley of the River Brett, which is
crossed by a little double hump-backed bridge. The timbered houses
and thatched cottages look much the same as when they were built,
and every year the village opens its gardens to the public.

Bildeston   *Map 2 ref E7*
14 miles W of Ipswich on the B1115

More fine old buildings here, including timber-framed cottages with
overhanging upper floors. The Church of St Mary has a superb carved
door and a splendid hammerbeam roof. A tablet inside the church
commemorates Captain Edward Rotherham, Commander of the
Royal Sovereign at the Battle of Trafalgar. He died in Bildeston while
staying with a friend and is buried in the churchyard.

Monks Eleigh   *Map 2 ref E7*
16 miles W of Ipswich on the A1141

The setting of thatched cottages, a 14th century church and a pump
on the village green is so traditional that Monks Eleigh was regularly used on railway posters as a lure to a wonderful part of the
country. The church at Brent Eleigh, on a side road off the A1141, is
remarkable for a number of quite beautiful ancient wall paintings,
discovered during maintenance work as recently as 1960. The most
striking and moving of the paintings is one of the Crucifixion.

Lavenham   *Map 2 ref D7*
18 miles W of Ipswich on the A1141

An absolute gem of a town, the most complete and original of the
medieval 'wool towns', with crooked timbered and whitewashed
buildings lining the narrow streets. From the 14th to the 16th centuries, Lavenham flourished as one of the leading wool and
cloth-making centres in the land, but with the decline of that industry the prosperous times soon came to an end. It is largely due to
the fact that Lavenham found no replacement industry that so much
of the medieval character remains: there was simply not enough
money for the rebuilding and development programmes that changed
many towns, often for the worse. The medieval street pattern still
exists, complete with market place and market cross.

Adrian and Pamela Palmer's **Prospect House** is an architect-
designed building dating from 1995 but blending harmoniously with
its older, often historic, neighbours in a quiet location a short distance from the market place. It's easy to spot with its round brick

Prospect House

corner and first-floor oriel window. For overnight guests there's a double bedroom with an adjoining bathroom and a small sitting room which has a single bed available for a third person in a family group. Breakfast is served in a large farmhouse-style kitchen/dining room. Prospect House is a non-smoking establishment. *Prospect House, Shilling Street, Lavenham, Suffolk, CO10 9RH. Tel: 01787 247496*

More than 300 buildings are officially listed as being of architectural and historical interest, and none of them is finer than the **Guildhall**. This superb 16th century timbered building was originally the meeting place of the Guild of Corpus Christi, an organisation that regulated the production of wool. It now houses exhibitions of local history and the wool trade, and its walled garden has a special area devoted to dye plants. **Little Hall** is hardly less remarkable, a 15th century hall house with a superb crown post roof. It was restored by the Gayer Anderson brothers, and has a fine collection of their furniture. The Church of St Peter and St Paul dominates the town from its elevated position. It's a building of great distinction, perhaps the greatest of all the 'wool churches' and declared by the 19th century architect August Pugin to be the finest example of Late Perpendicular style in the world. It was built, with generous help from wealthy local families (notably the Spryngs and the de Veres) in the late 15th and early 16th centuries to celebrate the end of the Wars of the Roses. Its flint tower is a mighty 140 feet in height and it's possible to climb to the top to take in the

Lavenham Guildhall

glorious views over Lavenham and the surrounding countryside. Richly carved screens and fine (Victorian) stained glass are eye-catching features within.

The Priory originated in the 13th century as a home for Benedictine monks and the beautiful timber-framed house on the site dates from about 1600. In the original hall, at the centre of the building, is an important collection of paintings and stained glass. The extensive grounds include a kitchen garden, a herb garden and a pond.

John Constable went to school in Lavenham, where one of his friends was Jane Taylor, who wrote *Twinkle Twinkle Little Star*.

The Six Bells is a 16th century building - originally three cottages - in a sleepy one-street village a short drive or a gentle, picturesque walk from Lavenham. It stands next to the Church of St Mary the Virgin and gained its name when the sixth bell was hung in the church in 1744. Owners Bob and Marilyn keep a set of hand bells in one of the bars, and guests are welcome to have a go or to play the piano. The scene in the bars and dining areas (extensive menus, including vegetarian and vegan, and well-kept cellar) is very English and traditional, with open fires, wood panelling and quarry-tiled floors, while outside there's a large car park, drinking places front and back, and an interactive animal area with horses, goats,

The Six Bells

hens, a cat and a dog. Five plots are available for campers and caravaners, and visitors arriving on horseback will find tethering facilities, hay and water before moseying on into the bar. *The Six Bells, The Street, Preston St Mary, Near Lavenham, Suffolk, CO10 9NG. Tel: 01787 247440*

Half a mile from Lavenham up a single-track lane, **Weaners Farm** enjoys a generous share of rural peace and quiet. There's hardly another building in sight, but at night Lavenham's floodlit church of St Peter and St Paul makes a spectacular and moving sight. The brick-built farmhouse is modern, with central heating, and the three bedrooms are light and airy, with great views over the rolling countryside. There's a large, well-appointed lounge with

Weaners Farm

books, TV and games, and a separate breakfast room. The extensive garden, sheltered by handsome trees and shrubs, is a perfect spot for relaxation, with benches and plenty of quiet little corners. *Weaners Farm, Bears Lane, Lavenham, Suffolk, CO10 9RX. Tel: 01787 247310*

Sudbury

Map 2 ref D8

21 miles W of Ipswich on the A131

Another wonderful town, the largest of the 'wool towns' and still home to a number of weaving concerns. Unlike Lavenham, it kept its industry because it was a port, and the result is a much more varied architectural picture. The surrounding countryside is some of the loveliest in Suffolk, and the River Stour is a further plus, with launch trips, rowing boats and fishing all available. Sudbury boasts three medieval churches, but what most visitors make a beeline for is **Gainsborough's House** on Market Hill. The painter Thomas Gainsborough was born here in 1727 in the house built by his father John. More of the artist's work is displayed in this Georgian-fronted house than in any other gallery, and there are also assorted 18th century memorabilia and furnishings. A changing programme of contemporary art exhibitions includes fine art, photography and sculpture and highlighting East Anglian artists in particular. A bronze statue of Gainsborough stands in the square.

About those churches: All Saints dates from the 15th century and has a glorious carved tracery pulpit and screens; 14th century St Gregory's is notable for a wonderful medieval font; and St Peter's has some marvellous painted screen panels and a piece of 15th century embroidered velvet.

Other buildings of interest are the **Victorian Corn Exchange**, now a library; **Salter's Hall**, a 15th century timbered house; and the **Quay Theatre**, a thriving centre for the arts.

CHAPTER SEVEN
Constable Country

River Stour at Flatford

Chapter 7 - Area Covered

For precise location of places please refer to the colour maps found at the rear of the book.

7
Constable Country

Introduction

England's greatest landscape painter was born at East Bergholt in 1776 and remained at heart a Suffolk man throughout his life. His father, Golding Constable, was a wealthy man who owned both Flatford Mill and Dedham Mill, the latter on the Essex side of the Stour. The river was a major source of inspiration to the young John Constable, and his constant involvement in country matters gave him an expert knowledge of the elements and a keen eye for the details of nature. He was later to declare "*I associate my careless boyhood with all that lies on the banks of the Stour. Those scenes made me a painter and I am grateful.*" That interest in painting developed early and was fostered by his friendship with John Dunthorne, a local plumber and amateur artist. He became a probationer at the Royal Academy Schools in 1799 and over the following years developed the technical skills to match his powers of observation. He painted the occasional portrait and even attempted a couple of religious works, but he concentrated almost entirely on the scenes that he knew and loved as a boy.

The most significant works of the earlier years were the numerous sketches in oil which were forerunners of the major paintings of Constable's mature years. He had exhibited at the Royal Academy every year since 1802, but it was not until 1817 that the first of his important canvases, *Flatford Mill on the River Stour*, was hung. This was succeeded by the six large paintings which became his best known works. These were all set on a short stretch of the Stour, and all except *The Hay Wain* show barges at work. These broad,

Flatford Mill

flat-bottomed craft were displayed in scenes remarkable for the realism of the colours, the effects of light and water and, above all, the beautiful depiction of clouds. His fellow-artist Fuseli declared that whenever he saw a Constable painting he felt the need to reach for his coat and umbrella. Though more realistic than anything that preceded them, Constable's paintings were never lacking soul, and his work was much admired by the painters of the French Romantic School. Two quotations from the man himself reveal much about his aims and philosophy:

"In a landscape I want to give one brief moment caught from fleeting time a lasting and sober existence."

And

"I never saw any ugly thing in my life; in fact, whatever may be the shape of an object, light, shade or perspective can always make it beautiful."

At the time of his death in 1837, Constable's reputation at home was relatively modest, though he had many followers and admirers in France. Awareness and understanding of his unique talent grew in the ensuing years, and his place as England's foremost landscape painter is rarely disputed.

Suffolk has produced many other painters of distinction. Thomas Gainsborough, born in Sudbury in 1727, was an artist of great versatility, innovative and instinctive, and equally at home with portraits and landscapes. He earned his living for a while from portrait painting in Ipswich before making a real name for himself in

Bath. His relations with the Royal Academy were often stormy, and in 1784 he had a major dispute over the height at which a painting should be hung. He withdrew his intended hangings from the exhibition and never again showed at the Royal Academy.

A man of equally indomitable spirit was Sir Alfred Munnings, born at Mendham in the north of Suffolk in 1878. The last of the great sporting painters, in the tradition of Stubbs and Marshall, Munnings was outspoken in his opinions of modern art. In 1949, as outgoing President of the Royal Academy, he launched an animated attack on modern art as 'silly daubs' and 'violent blows at nothing'. The occasion was broadcast on the radio and many listeners complained about the strong language used by Munnings. In 1956 he jolted the art world again by describing that year's Summer Exhibition as 'bits of nonsense' hung on the wall.

Mary Beale, born at Barrow in 1633, was a noted portrait painter and copyist; some of her work has been attributed to Lely and Kneller, and it was rumoured that Lely was in love with her.

Philip Wilson Steer (1860-1942) was among the most distinguished of the many painters who were attracted to Walberswick. He studied in Paris and acquired the reputation of being the best of the English impressionist painters.

The Suffolk tradition of painting continues to this day, with many artists drawn particularly to Walberswick and the beautiful Constable country. That beauty is not always easy to appreciate when crowds throng through the Stour valley at summer weekends, but at other times the peace and beauty are much as they were in Constable's day.

Capel St Mary   *Map 2 ref F8*
6 miles SW of Ipswich on the A12

Constable sketched here, but modern building has more or less overrun the old. A feature of the Church of St Mary is the weeping chancel, a slight kink between the nave and the chancel that apparently signifies Christ's head leaning to the right on the cross.

Brantham   *Map 2 ref F9*
8 miles SW of Ipswich on the A137

'Burnt Village' – possibly because it was sacked during a Danish invasion 1,000 years ago. The Church of St Michael owns one of the only two known religious paintings by Constable, *Christ Blessing the Children*, which he executed in the style of the American painter Benjamin West. It is kept in safety in Ipswich Museum. Just off the junction of the A137 and the B1070 is **Cattawade picnic site**, a small area on the edge of the Stour estuary. It's a good spot for birdwatching, and redshanks, lapwings and oystercatchers all breed on the well-known Cattawade Marshes. Fishing and canoeing are available, and there are public footpaths to Flatford Mill.

East Bergholt
8 miles SW of Ipswich off the A12

Map 2 ref F9

Narrow lanes lead to this picturesque and much visited little village. The **Constable County Trail** starts here, where the painter was born, and passes through Flatford Mill and on to Dedham in Essex. The actual house where he was born no longer stands, but the site is marked by a plaque on the fence of its successor, a private house called Constables. A little further along Church Street is Moss Cottage, which Constable once used as his studio. St Mary's Church is one of the many grand churches built with the wealth brought by the wool trade. This one should have been even grander, with a

St Mary's Church, East Bergholt

tower to rival that of Dedham across the river. The story goes that Cardinal Wolsey pledged the money to build the tower but fell from grace before the funds were forthcoming. The tower got no further than did his college in Ipswich, but a bellcage constructed in the churchyard as a temporary house for the bells became their permanent home, which it remains to this day. In this unique timber-framed structure the massive bells hang upside down and are rung by hand by pulling on the wooden shoulder stocks; an arduous task, as the five bells are among the heaviest in England. The church is naturally something of a shrine to Constable, his family and his friends. There are memorial windows to the artist and to his beloved wife Maria Bicknell, who bore him seven children and whose early death was an enormous blow to him. His parents, to whom he was clearly devoted, and his old friend Willy Lott, whose cottage is featured famously in *The Hay Wain*, are buried in the churchyard.

East Bergholt has an interesting mix of houses, some dating back as far as the 14th century. One of the grandest is **Stour House**, once the home of Randolph Churchill. Its gardens are open to the public, as is **East Berholt Place Garden** on the B1070 (Tel: 01206 299224).

A leafy lane leads south from the village to the Stour, where two of Constable's favourite subjects, **Flatford Mill** and **Willy Lott's cottage**, both looking much as they did when he painted them, are to be found. Neither is open to the public, and the brick watermill is run as a residential field study centre. Nearby Bridge Cottage at Flatford is a restored 16th century building housing a Constable display, a tea room and a shop. There's also a restored dry dock, and the whole area is a delight for walkers; it is easy to see how Constable drew constant inspiration from the wonderful riverside setting.

The Stour at Flatford

Stratford St Mary
Map 2 ref F9

10 miles SW of Ipswich just off the A12

Another of Constable's favourite locations, the most southerly village in Suffolk on the Essex border. *The Young Waltonians* and *A House in Water Lane* (the house still stands today) are the best known of his works set in this picturesque spot. The village church is typically large and imposing, with parts dating back to 1200. At the top of the village are two splendid half-timbered cottages called the **Ancient House** and the **Priest's House**. Stratford was once on the main coaching route to London, and the largest of the four pubs had stabling for 200 horses. It is claimed that Henry Williamson, author of *Tarka the Otter*, saw his first otter here.

Nayland
Map 2 ref E9

14 miles S of Ipswich on the B1087

On a particularly beautiful stretch of the Stour in Dedham Vale, Nayland has charming colour-washed cottages in narrow, winding streets, as well as two very fine 15th century buildings in Alston Court and the Guildhall. Abels Bridge, originally built of wood in the 15th century by wealthy merchant John Abel, divides Suffolk from Essex. In the 16th century a hump bridge replaced it, allowing barges to pass beneath, and the current bridge carries the original keystone bearing the initial A. In the Church of St James stands an altarpiece by Constable entitled *Christ Blessing the Bread and Wine.*

One mile west of Nayland, at the end of a track off the Bures road, stands the Norman Church of St Mary at Wissington. The church has a number of remarkable features, including several 13th century wall paintings, a finely carved 12th century doorway and a tiebeam and crown post roof.

Stoke by Nayland
Map 2 ref E9

12 miles SW of Ipswich on the B1087

The drive from Nayland reveals quite stunning views, and the village itself has a large number of listed buildings. The magnificent **Church of St Mary**, with its 120' tower, dominates the scene from its hilltop position; it dominated more than one Constable painting, the most famous showing the church lit up by a rainbow. William Dowsing destroyed 100 'superstitious pictures' here in his Puritan purges, but plenty of fine work is still to be seen, including several monumental brasses.

The Guildhall is another very fine building, now private residences but in the 16th century a busy centre of trade and commerce.

St Mary's Church, Stoke By Nayland

When the wool trade declined, so did the importance of the Guildhall, and for a time the noble building saw service as a workhouse.

The decline of the cloth trade in East Anglia had several causes. Fierce competition came from the northern and western weaving industries, which generally had easier access to water supplies for fulling; the wars on the continent of Europe led to the closure of some trading routes and markets; and East Anglia had no supplies of the coal that was used to drive the new steam-powered machinery. In some cases, as at Sudbury, weaving or silk took over as smaller industries.

Polstead   *Map 2 ref E9*
11 miles SW of Ipswich off the B1068

A very pretty village in wooded, hilly countryside, with thatched, colour-washed cottages around the green and a wide duck pond at the bottom of the hill. Standing on a rise above the pond are Polstead Hall, a handsome Georgian mansion, and the 12th century Church of St Mary. The church has two features not found elsewhere in Suffolk – a stone spire and the very early bricks used in its construction. The builders used not only these bricks, but also tiles and tufa, a soft, porous stone much used in Italy. In the grounds of the hall stand the remains of a 'Gospel Oak' said to have been 1,300 years old when it collapsed in 1953. Legend has it that Saxon missionaries preached beneath it in the 7th century; an open-air service is still held here annually.

Polstead has two other claims to fame. One is for Polstead Blacks, a particularly tasty variety of cherry which was cultivated in orchards around the village and which used to be honoured with an annual fair. The other is much less agreeable, for it was here that the notorious Red Barn murder hit the headlines in 1827. A young girl called Maria Marten, daughter of the local molecatcher, disappeared with William Corder, a farmer's son who was the girl's lover and father of her child. It was at first thought that they had eloped, but Maria's stepmother dreamt three times that she had been murdered and buried in a red barn. A search of the barn soon revealed this to be true. Corder was tracked down to Middlesex, tried and found guilty of Maria's murder and hanged. His skin was used to bind a copy of the trial proceedings and this, together with his scalp, is on display at Moyses Hall in Bury St Edmunds. The incident aroused a great deal of interest and today's visitors to the village will still find reminders of the ghastly deed: the thatched cottage where Maria lived stands, in what is now called Marten's Lane, and the farm where the murderer lived is now called Corder's Farm.

Boxford   Map 2 ref E8
12 miles W of Ipswich on the A1071

A gloriously unspoilt weaving village, downhill from anywhere, surrounded by the peaceful water meadows of the River Box. St Mary's Church dates back to the 14th century and its wooden north porch is one of the oldest of its kind in the country. In the church is a touching brass in memory of David Byrde, son of the rector, who died a baby in 1606. At the other end of the scale is Elizabeth Hyam, four times a widow, who died in her 113th year.

Hurrells Farmhouse is a fine old house, part Tudor part Jacobean, set in secluded grounds and gardens complete with a pond and a paddock for the owners' horses. Inside, the scene is equally appealing, with low beamed ceilings, inglenook, and tapestry wall hangings. Three beautifully furnished bedrooms provide neat, comfortable accommodation, and Aga-cooked breakfasts include eggs from Alok and Carol Deb's hens. Carol is exactly the right combination of host and friend, so guests will feel totally at home in her house (but they mustn't smoke!). There are resident cats and dogs, but house-trained pets are welcome. Horse-riding can be arranged for experienced riders. *Hurrells Farmhouse, Boxford Lane, Boxford, Near Sudbury, Suffolk, CO10 5JY. Tel: 01787 210215*

Hurrells Farmhouse

Bures

Map 2 ref D9

17 miles W of Ipswich on the B1508

At this point the River Stour turns sharply to the east, creating a natural boundary between Suffolk and Essex. The little village of Bures straddles the river, lying partly in each county. Bures St Mary in Suffolk is where the church is, overlooked by brick and half-timbered houses. Bures wrote itself very early into the history books when on Christmas Day 855 it is thought that our old friend Edmund the Martyr, the Saxon king, was crowned at the age of 15 in the Chapel of St Stephen. For some time after that momentous occasion Bures was the capital seat of the East Anglian kings. Bures has a long connection with the Waldegrave family, possibly from as far back as Chaucer's day. One of the Waldegrave memorials shows graphically the results of a visitation by Dowsing and the Puritan iconoclasts: all the figures of the kneeling children have had their hands cut off.

Tourist Information Centres

Centres in **bold** are open all the year around.

Aldeburgh
The Cinema, 51 High Street, Aldeburgh, Suffolk, IP15 5AU.
Tel/Fax: 01728 453637

Beccles
The Ouay, Fen Lane, Beccles, Suffolk NR34 9BH.
Tel/Fax: 01502 713196

Bury St Edmunds
6 Angel Hill, Bury St Edmunds, Suffolk IP33 1UZ.
Tel: 01284 764667 Fax: 01284 757084

Felixstowe
Leisure Centre, Sea Front, Felixstowe, Suffolk IP11 8AB.
Tel: 01394 276770 Fax: 01394 277456

Ipswich
St Stephen's Church, St Stephen's Lane, Ipswich, Suffolk IPl 1DP.
Tel: 01473 258070 Fax: 01473 258072

Lavenham
Lady Street, Lavenham, Suffolk CO10 9RA.
Tel: 01787 248207

Lowestoft
The East Point Pavilion, Royal Plain, Lowestoft
Suffolk NR33 OAP.   *Tel: 01502 523000 Fax: 01502 539023*

Newmarket
Palace House Mansion, Palace Street, Newmarket
Suffolk CB8 8EP.   *Tel: 01638 667200*

Southwold
Town Hall, Market Place, Southwold, Suffolk IP18 6EF.
Tel: 01502 724729 Fax: 01502 722978

Stowmarket, Mid-Suffolk
Wilkes Way, Stowmarket, Suffolk IP14 1DE.
Tel: 01449 676800 Fax: 01449 614691

Sudbury
Town Hall, Market Hill, Sudbury, Suffolk CO10 6TL.
Tel: 01787 881320

Woodbridge TIC
Station Buildings, Woodbridge, Suffolk IP12 4AJ
Tel/Fax: 01394 382240

Index

Y

The Hidden Places Series

ORDER FORM

To order more copies of this title or any of the others in this series
please complete the order form below and send to:

**Travel Publishing Ltd,7a Apollo House, Calleva Park
Aldermaston, Berks, RG7 8TN**

	Price	Quantity	Value
Regional Titles			
Cambridgeshire & Lincolnshire	£7.99	....	....
Channel Islands	£6.99	....	....
Cheshire	£7.99	....	....
Cornwall	£7.99	....	....
Devon	£7.99	....	....
Dorset, Hants & Isle of Wight	£4.95	....	....
Essex	£7.99	....	....
Gloucestershire	£6.99	....	....
Heart of England	£4.95	....	....
Highlands & Islands	£7.99	....	....
Kent	£7.99	....	....
Lake District & Cumbria	£7.99	....	....
Lancashire	£7.99	....	....
Norfolk	£7.99	....	....
Northeast Yorkshire	£6.99	....	....
Northumberland & Durham	£6.99	....	....
North Wales	£7.99	....	....
Nottinghamshire	£6.99	....	....
Peak District	£6.99	....	....
Potteries	£6.99	....	....
Somerset	£6.99	....	....
South Wales	£4.95	....	....
Suffolk	£7.99	....	....
Surrey	£6.99	....	....
Sussex	£6.99	....	....
Thames & Chilterns	£5.99	....	....
Warwickshire & West Midlands	£7.99	....	....
Welsh Borders	£5.99	....	....
Wiltshire	£6.99	....	....
Yorkshire Dales	£6.99	....	....
Set of any 5 Regional titles **£25.00**		....	....
National Titles			
England	£9.99	....	....
Ireland	£8.99	....	....
Scotland	£8.99	....	....
Wales	£8.99	....	....
Set of all 4 National titles **£28.00**		....	....
		_____	_____
TOTAL		_____	_____

**For orders of less than 4 copies please add £1 per book for
postage & packing. Orders over 4 copies P & P free.**

*PLEASE TURN OVER TO COMPLETE
PAYMENT DETAILS*

The Hidden Places Series
ORDER FORM

Please complete following details:

I wish to pay for this order by:

Cheque: ☐   Switch: ☐

Access: ☐   Visa: ☐

Either:

Card No: ☐☐☐☐ ☐☐☐☐ ☐☐☐☐ ☐☐☐☐

Expiry Date: ☐☐ ☐☐

Signature: ....

Or:

I enclose a cheque for £ .... made payable to Travel Publishing Ltd

NAME: ....

ADDRESS: ....

                             ....

                             ....

                             ....

POSTCODE: ....

TEL NO: ....

Please send to: Travel Publishing Ltd
7a Apollo House
Calleva Park
Aldermaston
Berks, RG7 8TN

The Hidden Places Series
READER REACTION FORM

The Hidden Places research team would like to receive reader's comments on any visitor attractions or places reviewed in the book and also recommendations for suitable entries to be included in the next edition. This will help ensure that the *Hidden Places* series continues to provide its readers with useful information on the more interesting, unusual or unique features of each attraction or place ensuring that their stay in the local area is an enjoyable and stimulating experience.

To provide your comments or recommendations would you please complete the forms below as indicated and send to: **The Research Department, Travel Publishing Ltd., 7a Apollo House, Calleva Park, Aldermaston, Reading, RG7 8TN.**

Please tick as appropriate: Comments ☐ Recommendation ☐

Name of *"Hidden Place"*:

Address:

Telephone Number:

Name of Contact:

Comments/Reason for recommendation:

Name of Reader:

Address:

Telephone Number:

Map Section

The following pages of maps encompass the main cities, towns and geographical features of Suffolk as well as all the many interesting places featured in the guide. Distances are indicated by the use of scale bars located below each of the maps

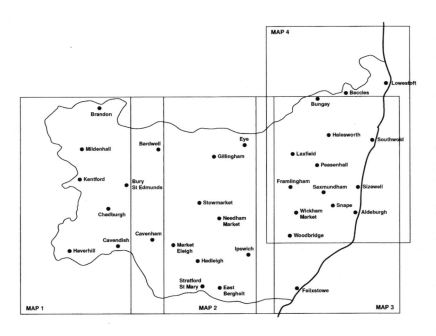

These maps are small scale extracts from the *East Anglia Official Tourist Map,* reproduced with kind permission of *Estates Publications.*

MAP 1

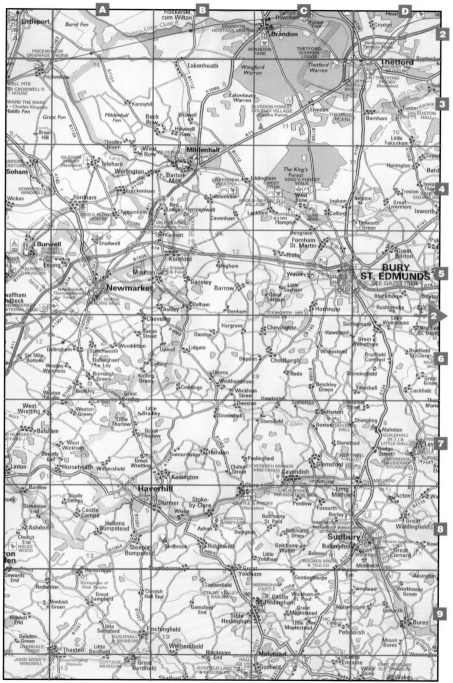

MAP 2

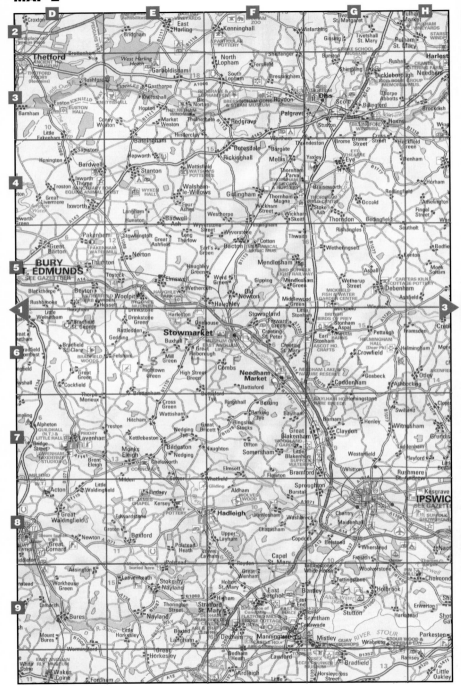

MAP 3

MAP 4

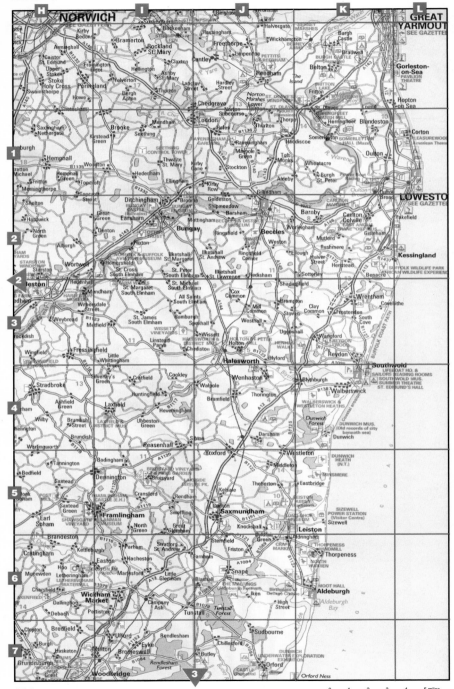

©Estate Publications   Crown Copyright Reserved